SHAKESPEARE AND ITALY

by

ERNESTO GRILLO
M.A., D.LIT., LL.D., D.C.L.

HASKELL HOUSE PUBLISHERS LTD.
Publishers of Scarce Scholarly Books
NEW YORK, N.Y. 10012
1973

822.33
FG859s

HASKELL HOUSE PUBLISHERS LTD.
Publishers of Scarce Scholarly Books
280 LAFAYETTE STREET
NEW YORK, N. Y. 10012

Library of Congress Cataloging in Publication Data

Grillo, Ernesto, 1877-1946.
   Shakespeare and Italy.

   Reprint of the 1949 ed. privately printed by R. Maclehose, University Press, Glasgow.
   1. Shakespeare, William, 1564-1616—Knowledge—Italy. 2. Shakespeare, William, 1564-1616—Appreciation—Italy. 3. Italy—Relations (general) with Great Britain. 4. Great Britain—Relations (general) with Italy. I. Title.
PR3069.I8G7   1973   822.3'3   73-10197
ISBN 0-8383-1719-7

78-7584
Printed in the United States of America

Library of
Davidson College

SHAKESPEARE AND ITALY

PREFACE

This modest volume is offered as a sincere, though utterly inadequate, tribute to the memory of a great and beloved teacher. It is therefore hoped that the reader will indulgently overlook its shortcomings, as it has been compiled mainly from Professor Grillo's own Lecture Notes, often fragmentary and mostly in Italian.

In order to re-evoke as far as possible the atmosphere of the class-room no attempt has been made to produce a dogmatic textbook, since it was ever the lecturer's chief aim to stimulate his students to further literary research.

Grateful thanks are due to Professor Grillo's relatives in Italy for their interest and encouragement, especially to Monsignor Can. Prof. Don Michele Grillo (from whose *Alta Irpinia* historical details have been gleaned), to Professor R. P. Cowl and Mrs. Elizabeth Y. Whitley (*née* Thom) for permission to print extracts from their speeches and to Mr. A. W. Macdonald for assistance in the revision of proofs.

GLASGOW, *February*, 1949.

CONTENTS

	PAGE
INTRODUCTION	11
CULTURAL RELATIONS BETWEEN BRITAIN AND ITALY	39
SHAKESPEARE AND ITALY	
HIS SOURCES OF INSPIRATION AND MATERIAL	87
SHAKESPEARE AND HIS ITALIAN CRITICS	99
SHAKESPEARE ON THE ITALIAN STAGE	108
DID SHAKESPEARE KNOW ITALIAN?	125
DID SHAKESPEARE VISIT ITALY?	132
GEOGRAPHY OF ITALY IN SHAKESPEARIAN DRAMA	141

ILLUSTRATIONS

Ernesto Grillo   *Frontispiece*

Waterways of Lombardy   ,,   ,,   144

INTRODUCTION

For some years prior to 1939 the deterioration in Anglo-Italian relations had made inexpedient the publication in Britain of works relating to Italian Literature; but at the time of Professor Grillo's sudden death, a year after the cessation of hostilities, he hopefully anticipated an early return to conditions more favourable for the appearance of some, at least, of the results of his research in the field of Comparative Literature—a subject to which he had long devoted a major portion of his time and energy. It may not now be practicable to publish all that he himself intended, but the present volume, designed primarily to recall to former students the happy hours spent in his Lecture Room, may also serve to introduce him to a less academic public, since its subject matter is of more general interest. It has been felt, too, that both classes of readers might be glad to have a few facts regarding the author's life and personality—his work speaks for itself.

Between the mediaeval Castle and the ancient Cathedral of S. Angelo dei Lombardi, South Italy, stands Casa Grillo where, on 2nd December, 1876, to Don Vincenzo Grillo, 'nobile gentiluomo,' and his wife, Donna Maria Ripandelli, was born a third son, whom they named Ernesto Nicola Giuseppe. For many centuries the Grillo family had owned extensive estates in the neighbourhood and had proved themselves

INTRODUCTION

valiant warriors in the military operations of so frequent occurrence in the history of Alta Irpinia—a province which had undergone many changes of fortune even before the Roman Occupation. In his *History Of The Noble Families Of Southern Italy* (Vol. VI) Count Gonzaga relates the story, from 1100 onwards, of many of the Grillo family, including Ansaldo, who led the Genoese army against the forces of Pisa in 1158, Giovanni, the trusted counsellor of Queen Joanna I, whom she sent as her ambassador to Pope Urban VI at Avignon, and Angelo, the learned Abbot of Monte Cassino, who was a friend of Tasso. In more recent times members of the Grillo and Ripandelli families have occupied positions of eminence in Church and State, in Literature and Medicine. It may therefore be assumed that from both sides Ernesto inherited outstanding intellectual gifts.

Apart from his parents, the relative who took the greatest interest in his upbringing was his uncle, the saintly Don Carmine Grillo, whose ambition it was to see his favourite nephew follow a clerical career. Accordingly, the child was sent at an early age to a seminary where the pupils were obliged to assume priestly garb. Here the discipline was rigid in the extreme and particularly irksome to such a high-spirited boy as Don Ernestino undoubtedly was. On his own admission he was the 'enfant terrible' of the family (whom everyone loved in spite of his naughtiness), and the ringleader in every kind of mischief, in school and out of it. His democratic tendencies were early apparent, for even the most exalted personages

INTRODUCTION

who came on a visit to Casa Grillo enjoyed no immunity from his practical jokes. One historic escapade literally left its mark on him to the end of his days. On this occasion he and his fellow 'abatini' were engaged in some pursuit contrary to the rules of the school, when they suddenly saw approaching the severely dignified figure of Rector Maffei, later Bishop of Lacedonia. The other culprits took the most obvious means of escape; but Ernesto, with his usual resourcefulness, climbed into a huge grandfather clock situated on the landing. Unfortunately, this unaccustomed addition to the 'works' upset the balance of the clock, which somersaulted down the staircase. When discovered he was found to have sustained such severe injuries that he lay unconscious for days afterwards. While still a seminarist he took to writing verse in which he burlesqued doctors, artists, nuns and prelates. These satires were not published at the time for fear of offending the victims or their families, but the fragments which have been preserved make entertaining reading even now. In addition to this literary relaxation he wrote serious articles for a provincial journal—*L'Eco dell'Ofanto*—in particular an interesting series on 'La Libertà Cattolica'.

Whether it was his accident, or the constant restrictions and impositions to which he had to submit, cannot now be said with certainty, but before long the 'young abbot' decided that a clerical life held no attraction for him. Fortunately his relatives did not insist; so, at the age of eighteen, he laid aside his ecclesiastical vestments and proceeded to the Royal

INTRODUCTION

Liceo-Ginnasio at Foggia, where he obtained his licentiate diploma. In both seminary and liceo-ginnasio he was invariably first in his class, carrying off many medals and prizes—a prelude to the notable academic successes he was later to enjoy in numerous Italian and foreign universities. Among the degrees he obtained before leaving Italy were LL.D. and D.C.L. —granted there for merit, in contrast to the formal and arbitrary way in which such degrees are sometimes conferred elsewhere.

At S. Angelo dei Lombardi, Don Vincenzo Grillo, a cultured and broad-minded gentleman, had employed English tutors and governesses, so that his family should early acquire a sound knowledge of our language and literature. As his sons reached adolescence he sent them to spend their summer vacation in the home of some well-known Englishman. Of all the brothers Ernesto seems to have been specially attracted towards the British way of life; which is all the more surprising since his 'guardian', a conscientious and highly respected clergyman of the Church of England, forbade him to accept any invitations to social functions from which he could not be relied upon to return before 6 p.m.! This incarceration of a lively youth of sixteen during the long evenings of an English summer was a thing Ernesto Grillo never forgot; and later, when he himself came to have a share in the training of young people, it gave him much pleasure to note the changed attitude of twentieth-century educationists. Remembering Rector Maffei as well as the Victorian martinet he used to exclaim, 'How severely I was punished for

INTRODUCTION

doing the very things for which children nowadays receive high praise'.

At the outbreak of the Boer War he was studying at Bonn University; but, incensed at the insulting remarks made about England by his professors and fellow-students, he impulsively decided to sever all connection with Germany and to sail immediately for England, where he was to spend one of the happiest periods of his life studying at St. John's College, Cambridge. At the age of twenty-six he was appointed Professor of English and German in the University of Urbino, where he remained until 1905, when he became Director of the Anglo-American Institute in Florence. During his stay of about five years there he identified himself wholeheartedly with the religious, social and cultural activities of the English-speaking community, entertaining on a lavish scale distinguished visitors to the enchanting City of Flowers, some of whom he later numbered among his colleagues and friends in Scotland.

In 1910, seeking a complete change of scene after a tragic personal disillusionment, Professor Grillo decided to accept a post offered him in Glasgow University by its Principal and Vice-Chancellor, the late Sir Donald MacAlister, K.C.B. This apparently reckless decision surprised and disappointed his Italian friends, who had foreseen for him a brilliant career in his native land, not only in the sphere of literature but also in that of politics; for by this time he was already famed for the eloquence of his political oratory. It must be said, however, that, although he came to Scotland of his own volition, he intended to make only a brief stay; and no one was more astonished than himself that he should ultimately choose to remain under our grey northern skies for the rest of his life.

When, in October 1910, Ernesto Grillo arrived in Glasgow for his installation as Head of the Department of Italian Language and Literature, a position he held until 1940, he found a department consisting of one solitary student! Yet by the unbounded enthusiasm, energy and indefatigable exertions of its Head it was destined to increase a thousandfold—an achievement all the more notable because this increase in the number of students of Italian and, *ipso facto*, of friends of Italy, was in inverse proportion to the cordiality of Anglo-Italian political relations during this period. That the outstanding success of the department was entirely due to his own personality and hard work was a conclusion which even he, modest though he essentially was, could not fail to reach; and in a letter dated 3rd June, 1927, he says: 'From my arrival here until now I have spent quite a fortune of my own. Italian is not studied in the schools, and the whole department is my own creation. When I first came there was only one student, and I did not mean to stay, but I had promised the government of my own country and the British authorities to do my best, so I got to work—*I love to attack and to conquer the impossible*—and now after many years of hard work and many, many sacrifices there is a Department. But the question is how long it will remain thus when I am gone.' There can be little doubt of the answer to that question.

INTRODUCTION

From his earliest days Ernesto Grillo had been of a studious disposition, and for many years after finally settling in Britain he spent a good part of every University vacation following his bent for research in the congenial atmosphere of the British Museum. To a friend privileged to collaborate with him in much of his literary work he wrote at Easter, 1930: 'I am working almost all day at the Museum; for want of your help and co-operation my work is delayed for at least two years ... I am sorry to have given you so much trouble with the translation of your lecture notes.' (Subsequently published as *Studies in Modern Italian Literature*.) 'If I had only realised how I was sacrificing you I should never have asked you to do it. But often many of the things I say in class are not in my notes and these improvisations are far more precious to me than the prepared lectures.' Even when he forsook the Reading Room for a brief stay in the country (preferably East Anglia) he had little real leisure, for he continued to write countless letters to, or on behalf of, his students. On one such occasion, writing from the vicinity of Bicester, he says, 'Do not imagine that I have had much rest. It is true that I am not lecturing, but I can tell you that a few hours' shooting and the letters I have written to you have been my only pleasures during these weeks.'

How arduously he worked even on vacation may be judged by the lengthy, though incomplete, list of his published works (to be found in *Who's Who* up till the year of his death): ranging from *De Luci Acci Vita et Scriptis* and *De Joanne Cassiano*, contributions to

INTRODUCTION

Latin literature which earned him international awards, to his lucid New Italian Grammar and his Elementary Readers, *La Dolce Favella* and *Gemme e Fiori*. His two volumes on Early Italian Authors were mainly intended for students of mediaeval literature, but thousands have been indebted to his *Italian Poets* and *Prose Writers* for their introduction to the life and work of authors from Guinizelli to D'Annunzio and from St. Francis to Fogazzaro.

Few university professors can have led such a strenuous life in term time as Professor Grillo, for he delivered more lectures per week and addressed larger audiences than did most of his colleagues; and however often he might have lectured previously on the author under discussion his lectures were always freshly prepared and the subject generally viewed from a new angle. In this way neither he nor his lectures were ever 'stale'. But this practice involved an immense amount of work ungrudgingly undertaken because he was ever an idealist and considered nothing but the best worth offering to his students. And it was not those of Glasgow and Edinburgh Universities alone who came under his irresistible spell and benefited from his painstaking researches. During the summers of 1928-30 he acquired an international reputation through the brilliant courses of lectures he delivered at the Royal University for Foreigners in Perugia. It is said that in spite of intense heat the hall was invariably crowded, and the enthusiasm of his cultured audience 'beyond description'. Indeed many of these students—some of them scholars of renown in their own countries—are

INTRODUCTION

reputed to have made the journey from the U.S.A. and elsewhere solely for the privilege of attending his lectures, which he polished and re-polished till the moment of delivery. 'This morning I was up at four and worked till nine revising what we wrote in Norfolk.'

Previous to settling in Scotland Professor Grillo had, in addition to his estates in South Italy, owned a house in the neighbourhood of Perugia. On returning there in 1928 his pleasure at meeting old friends like Count Anzidei, who presided at his lectures, was mingled with sadness. 'I miss so very many who are no longer alive. Here in Perugia everything has changed during these last few years. Wealth has passed into the hands of Jews and speculators. This morning I took a walk out into the country to see my lovely villa, which I sold about twenty years ago. It was heartbreaking to see the terrible transformation: the woods cut down, the garden a wilderness, the walls in disrepair and the house itself converted into a brewery.'

At the Royal University for Foreigners, Perugia, most of his lectures were on Comparative Literature, in which study he was a pioneer. Indeed the courses which he inaugurated soon after his arrival in Glasgow were among the first to be held in any modern university. Since he considered familiarity with an outline of European literature an indispensable preliminary to the study of English literature, it seems appropriate to include in this volume a translation of the brief sketch of Cultural Relations between Italy and Great Britain, which he prepared for the benefit of his compatriots living in this country and which was published in the

INTRODUCTION

Guida Generale Degli Italiani In Gran Bretagna of 1939.

When Professor Grillo visited Italy in the summer of 1929 he suffered many indignities at the hands of Fascist officials, including the confiscation of his passport and other papers—a procedure evidently intended to prevent his return to Britain. But, to quote his own words in another connection, 'all the obstacles in the world will never make me change my mind,' so he immediately set about planning his escape across the frontier into the wilds of Albania and through half the countries of Europe. After undergoing untold hardships on this perilous journey he eventually reached England ragged, bruised and penniless but triumphant though with little expectation of ever seeing his beloved homeland again. The disastrous earthquake of the following year, however, caused such severe damage to his house and estate near S. Angelo that it was imperative that he should go and arrange for urgent repairs to his property. Permission was granted him to pay a brief visit, and on this occasion he was unmolested. In the course of a public lecture delivered in Glasgow in the autumn of the same year he remarked that the damage caused by the earthquake was far more extensive than press notices indicated. This being duly reported to Rome, he was severely censured by the Fascist Government for his implied criticism of the régime. From then till the outbreak of war they never ceased to penalise him for his anti-fascist views in any way possible to them, e.g. surveillance of his every movement by spies (Italian and British) and interference

INTRODUCTION

with his correspondence. So thorough was their organisation that this persecution was even extended to some of his Scottish friends, who had never evinced the slightest interest in Italian politics. Notwithstanding all this, but doubtless with some ulterior motive, the Italian government conferred upon him in June, 1939, the title of Knight Officer of the Crown of Italy. When in 1940 the long-dreaded blow fell influential Italians, including the Ambassador and the Consul General, used all their powers of persuasion and intimidation in an attempt to make him return to Italy with them. In vain they tried to convince him of the imminent annihilation of Britain; he never wavered in his resolve and declared, in terms which to them must have been incomprehensible, his fixed determination to share whatever fate might befall the Scottish friends to whom he was wholeheartedly devoted.

It was indeed a sad day for him when the diplomatic liner sailed from the Clyde, for with it departed his long-cherished hopes of a reconciliation between the two countries he loved so dearly and for whose good relations he had striven unceasingly. Since 1930 he had been debarred even from visiting his aged father; now he was fated never to see any member of his family again. At the end of August, 1940, he heard from the Apostolic Nuncio that Cardinal Maglione, Vatican Secretary of State, was pleased to hear that all his friends and the Scottish people at large had been so kind to him throughout the trying days which followed Italy's entry into the war.

Having made his decision to remain in Scotland,

INTRODUCTION

Professor Grillo lost no time in futile repining. For him there was no turning back; he literally put his hand to the plough and, with a mind too distraught for literary work, concentrated all his efforts upon increasing food production at Asker, so beautifully situated on the hills above Cardross and commanding magnificent views of Loch Lomond and the Firth of Clyde. Here he conducted some noteworthy experiments in the eradication of bracken on hill land. The best of methods practised by professional agriculturists with mechanical cutters seem merely to reduce the pest to manageable proportions, but Professor Grillo's scheme of intensive cutting by hand over a period of two, or at most three, seasons resulted in its complete extermination. In this way he reclaimed many acres of unproductive land and, but for the increasing labour shortage due to the war, would undoubtedly have accomplished much more. It ought perhaps to be said that the success of his experiment may have been partly due to the fact that the Professor himself worked along with the local lads he employed, inspiring them with his own prodigious enthusiasm and thoroughness to persevere in a task which otherwise they might have carried out in a much more perfunctory manner.

His interest in country life was not however confined to agriculture. He was a tireless climber, a fearless rider and a crack shot. Paradoxically he loved birds and animals though he shot them. His marksmanship being so good, they seldom suffered. On the very rare occasions when his shot did not kill instantaneously, he would persist in his search till he found the wounded victim

INTRODUCTION

and put an end to its suffering. He had no sympathy with sportsmen who are content to remain in the butts waiting for a bird to come their way. For him shooting meant tramping for hours with gun and dogs, whether it was in the crisp autumn air over the moors of Dunbartonshire or under the blazing sun on the mountains of S. Angelo. At such times his powers of physical endurance were proverbial, and he could out-walk any of his gamekeepers. During his last visit to Italy, in September, 1930, he wrote: 'For the last three days I have been shooting in extreme heat. Two men who accompanied me fainted yesterday and I had to get help to bring them as far as the high road where the car was waiting for us.' And the following week: 'Last Saturday I went shooting on the mountains of Guardia Lombardi (3,400 ft.) and came in contact with a ravenous wolf attacking half a dozen sheep. He had already killed one and was dragging it through the ravines despite the shouting of the shepherd. I shot him but was unable to kill him because the small pellets failed to pierce his skin. He left the sheep and, like a barking dog, turned towards me only to get two more shots at shorter range. Shooting here is a very toilsome task. Imagine going up and down through a range of mountains higher than Ben Nevis and you will have a little idea of what it means. You will be glad to hear that nobody can beat me for walking and all declare that my legs are made of iron. I am quite well despite the labours of ascending and descending, which have only had the effect of hardening my limbs and reducing my weight.'

INTRODUCTION

In the country too he derived much pleasure from entertaining numerous friends and acquaintances. He was an ideal host and nothing gave him greater delight than to see his guests enjoying a meal cooked by himself. Much as he loved and admired Britain, his admiration did not extend to her cuisine, as he experienced it in most private houses and hotels. After a particularly unappetising and indigestible repast he was once heard to exclaim in a tone unusually critical, 'O England, land of bottled sauces and patent medicines!' It is no exaggeration to say that a 'frittata', 'crema' or 'zabaglione' prepared by him was a revelation to many who considered themselves capable cooks. In this, as in everything else, he was unobtrusively methodical; and a bachelor friend who spent an occasional week-end with him at Asker used to say, 'I never cease to wonder at the rapidity and total absence of fuss with which he produces a marvellous meal.' The Professor loved good food and good wine, not so much as a satisfaction to himself, for he was truly abstemious, but as a means of giving pleasure to others. On one of his last visits to his old home in S. Angelo he wrote to a friend in Scotland: 'I am well and have put on weight. I shall have to give up eating, but I shall continue to drink every day a good flask of old moscato, which I am so sorry I cannot share with you.'

Nor were his domestic accomplishments purely culinary. Ever a firm believer in conscription, he held that compulsory training was especially beneficial to youths of the upper classes, teaching them to be self-reliant and independent of the services of others. As

INTRODUCTION

far as he was concerned, there was nothing he could not do for himself—darning, mending and even laundry-work, when domestic help became unobtainable during the war. Whatever he undertook he did with boundless enthusiasm and did it superlatively well; he had to confess; however, that in his earliest attempts at darning, his excess of zeal to fill up the holes led to results which were sometimes 'rather lumpy'.

Though he preferred a quiet country life yet, like most Italians, he could also enjoy the bustle of the city. This was especially true of London, where in his earlier years he spent part of every vacation. While there he made his headquarters at the Savage Club, of which he was proud to be a member and where he enjoyed the congenial company of the foremost literary men of the day. He liked to recall how, as a very small child in Italy, he had sat upon the knee of Robert Browning himself—an incident which augured well for his future interest in English literature. While in London he rarely made use of bus or Tube, preferring to walk from his club to the Museum or to any other destination however distant. In this way he acquired an unrivalled knowledge of the streets and by-ways of the city. It was a coveted treat to accompany him on one of his explorations of Soho, for example, where one could spend hours without hearing a word of English, and then to share with him an unusual but perfectly cooked and supremely appetising meal in some Italian restaurant, apparently obscure but none the less the rendezvous of connoisseurs.

INTRODUCTION

In Glasgow, too, he was an indefatigable pedestrian; but here his walks were often undertaken for some charitable purpose. He had a genius for making friends, and, though mindful and proud of his noble ancestry, he had not the slightest trace of snobbishness in his nature or of patronage in his manner. No home, Italian or British, was too humble for him to enter; and to many in poverty or affliction his friendship was a veritable 'green hill by the side of life's dusty road'. He never arrived empty-handed, and the value of his gifts was often enhanced by real personal sacrifice, especially during the war when delicacies were wellnigh unobtainable. His unselfish consideration and his winsome tenderness endeared him to many chronic invalids, to whom his visits were a source of infinite joy and comfort. Countless members of the younger generation, too, owed him an incalculable debt of gratitude for his understanding assistance. One of the saddest episodes of his life occurred as he was walking one winter evening with his golden retriever in Kelvingrove Park. He was approached by a young woman who, after accosting him, fled precipitately, but not before he had recognised her as one of his own students. He recalled the embarassed girl and enquired into the circumstances which had brought her there. On learning that she and her widowed mother were in arrears with their rent, without hesitation he offered to make himself responsible for their debts, if she would promise never again to resort to such a course of action. The student did not fail to collect the money as arranged the following morning, but whether her tale was true or whether she

INTRODUCTION

subsequently kept her promise he had no means of knowing. As he said, 'It is better to believe too much than too little'; and on another occasion, writing of one who had betrayed his trust, 'In this world it is better to suffer wicked deeds than to do them. Thus one has at least the satisfaction of having done one's duty.'

His rare periods of complete relaxation Professor Grillo liked to spend in bracing sea air, choosing for preference a quiet resort on the shores of East Anglia or, in later years, on the Carrick coast. There his pleasures were childlike in their simplicity, and he was unsurpassed in his faculty for sharing the joys and sorrows of ordinary people. Social functions or the so-called 'popular' entertainment of theatre or radio had little attraction for him, though he would occasionally wander through a Fair Ground watching children, for whom he had the deepest affection, enjoying the merry-go-rounds and other amusements. He was not himself a musician nor had he any profound knowledge of the composers of countries other than his own, but he had a good ear and a fondness for Italian Opera and Folk Music, particularly songs in the Neapolitan dialect. He loved too the old English Christmas Carols and some of the great hymns of the Church.

One of his favourite pastimes at the seaside was that of putting pennies in slot machines—especially those that tell one's weight and character! He used to laugh at the latter and promptly throw away the cards. One, however, dated Lowestoft 22. 3. 31 he sent to a friend, remarking that it might have been made expressly for him. It reads, 'You have strong abilities, but have also

INTRODUCTION

a fiery, impetuous nature. Learn to curb this. It is your only fault.' It is interesting to note that he considered this a just estimate of his character; and certainly his bitterest opponent could say nothing worse of him; for he was far from being one of those colourless individuals of whom it can be said that they 'never made an enemy'. Indeed, in the first few years of his stay in Glasgow, he was in constant danger of being stabbed to death by some of his compatriots, because of his avowed disapproval of certain of their business practices, which he considered a blot on the fair name of Italy. His concern with the physical and moral welfare of both employees and customers earned him the esteem of the majority but the hostility of an unscrupulous minority among the traders. In his successful efforts to clean up, literally and metaphorically, the ice-cream shops of Glasgow and neighbourhood he received the whole-hearted support of the Police Force, with whose Aliens' Department he was always on the best of terms.

Another notable instance of this friendly co-operation occurred some ten years later, when a valuable Byzantine Processional Cross was found in Glasgow, displayed for sale in the shop of a second-hand dealer, to whom it had been sold by an Italian from Aquila, who claimed to have discovered it amongst the ruins of Messina after the earthquake. The cross, which was twenty-two inches high, had apparently been smuggled out of Italy in pieces, and when re-assembled answered to the description of one stolen from a church in Borgocollefegato and valued at £42,000. Accordingly, in July, 1921, Professor Grillo, then Acting Consul General,

INTRODUCTION

raised an action in the Sheriff Court for the restitution of the cross. The Sheriff decreed that evidence of its identification must be obtained in Rome; so in February, 1922, Inspector (later Superintendent) McCaskill of the Aliens' Department, City of Glasgow Police, made a special journey to Italy, taking the cross with him. The evidence being indisputable, this interesting ecclesiastical relic was restored to the church and the native of Aquila extradited.

Few Glasgow professors did more than he to promote an *entente cordiale* between Town and Gown. Too much of an individualist and too restlessly impatient of fruitless discussions to be 'a good committee-man', his means and his talents as a lecturer were freely at the disposal of every good cause; and many an obscure society in the west of Scotland had reason to be grateful to him for his revelation of the wonders of Italian art and literature. Even to the humblest and most unlettered audience he gave of his best and they, in their turn, never failed to respond to the glowing cordiality of his manner and the irresistible friendliness of his smile. He had the rare and enviable gift of radiating happiness wherever he went; but, with eyes flashing in fierce indignation, he could be impressively eloquent in his denunciation of injustice or treachery; and it would have surprised most of his friends to know that his habitually sunny disposition was sometimes overshadowed by dark clouds of depression. That so very few even suspected the physical and mental tortures he suffered at these times is an indication of the superb courage with which he practised the noble injunction:

INTRODUCTION

'Fais énergiquement ta longue et lourde tâche
Dans la voie où le sort a voulu t'appeler,
Puis, après, comme moi, souffre et meurs sans parler'.

When Professor Grillo died very unexpectedly at Girvan, on 6th July, 1946, many friends found it impossible to attend his funeral there. It was therefore thought fitting to give them an opportunity of paying their respects at the unveiling of a monument to him in Doune Cemetery, on 18th October, 1947. The service of dedication was conducted by the Rev. Prof. Wm. Fulton, D.D., LL.D., and the memorial unveiled by the Italian Consul, Dr. P. L. Alverà, who also, prior to the ceremony, at a Lunch attended by representatives of Glasgow University and numerous other public bodies, read messages from Professor Grillo's relatives in Italy, the Mayor and citizens of S. Angelo dei Lombardi and the Metropolitan Archbishop of Conza. Tributes were paid by Professor Fulton who presided, by Professor R. P. Cowl, an intimate friend and former colleague and by Mrs. Elizabeth Whitley, a former student.

In the course of his speech Professor Cowl said: 'It is now more than thirty years since I first had the privilege of meeting Professor Grillo in the house of a mutual friend. Still a comparatively young man in the full vigour of his powers, he was then engaged in the task of creating a Department of Italian Studies in the University of Glasgow. That he should succeed in building up so flourishing a department was no slight achievement in a period in which Italian received little recognition or encouragement from British universities.

INTRODUCTION

In most of them Italian may be said to have been a Cinderella among her sister languages, and Departments of Italian were either non-existent or attracted a very small number of students. It was not so, however, in Glasgow, where the Professor of Italian happened to be a man of exceptional energy, who endeared himself to the students by his eloquence, his gifts of humour and sympathy, and, above all, by his passion to impart his knowledge to his listeners, and to communicate to them his own infectious enthusiasm for letters and the arts. He lectured brilliantly on the great writers of Italy from Dante to Leopardi; and, happily inspired, he instituted courses of lectures on what he called Comparative Literature. In these lectures he dwelt upon the many contacts between the Italian and English literatures from the Age of Chaucer to that of Byron and Shelley. He was one of the first to lay stress upon the influence of the Commedia dell'Arte on the nascent English Theatre of the sixteenth century, and he was alone in making the suggestion that Shakespearian drama displayed an acquaintance with the Italian scene and an insight into the Italian soul that could only have been gained from a personal knowledge of the country, its people and literature. There was at the time little concrete evidence to support this suggestion, and Shakespearian scholars held strongly the tradditional view that Shakespeare had "small Latin and less Greek" and no knowledge of any modern literature save the English. Students of Dante had noted parallels in Shakespeare to thoughts or images in the *Divine Comedy*, but these were too few and

INTRODUCTION

too slight in themselves to have much weight as evidence.

'Professor Grillo made some valuable contributions to Shakespearian scholarship, offering, for instance, a most ingenious solution to one of the most mystifying allusions in all Shakespeare. You will remember how Malvolio, in *Twelfth Night*, was mischievously hoaxed into believing that his mistress, the Lady Olivia, was in love with him, her steward. In a day-dream he is contemplating his good fortune. Why should he not aspire to a marriage with the Countess? There was example for it, "the Lady of the Strachy married the yeoman of the wardrobe". Now no one had ever been able to throw any light upon the identity of the Lady of the Strachy until Professor Grillo wrote: "In view of the dramatist's love for everything Italian, and of the Italian source and flavour of *Twelfth Night*, is it not possible to derive 'Strachy' from the Italian *stracci*—i.e. rags? 'The Lady of the Strachy' is, in fact, the English rendering of the Italian, *La Signora degli Stracci*, a sarcasm still common in many parts of Italy in allusion to a lady poor but haughty. 'Strachy' may reasonably be a corruption or a phonetic adaptation of *stracci*, for in Shakespeare we meet with a large number of Italian names and words anglicised. Either a play of words is intended between *The Lady of the Strachy*—i.e. of the rags—and 'the yeoman of the wardrobe', or it is even possible that the dramatist meant to allude to the authentic romance of some poor but proud lady who married a yeoman of the wardrobe."

'Professor Grillo's School of Italian Studies has

INTRODUCTION

proved its usefulness, and it may serve as a model for similar schools in other universities, when, as will happen, a knowledge of Italian comes to be recognised as an indispensable part of the equipment of every serious student of English literature.'

In a most moving tribute expressing on behalf of former students 'some of the great debt of gratitude we all owe to Professor Grillo for his teaching—and so much more than his teaching' Mrs. Whitley said: 'What makes one's University years so fascinating and yet so fearful is that there for the first time Youth with its dreams and ideals comes to grips with materialism and the grey utilities of life. What gratitude then is adequate from a student to a teacher who had the genius to proclaim that it was the Golden World that was the Reality, the leaden one that was the counterfeit, the shadow; who had the courage to maintain his own vision undimmed and his own enthusiasm unabated, despite all the disappointments and mischances that life can bring; who kept his integrity unconquered, his spirit as free of the bars of materialism as a bird out of the fowler's snare? The Professor's favourite line of Shakespeare, so often quoted to us was: "This above all—To thine own self be true." . . . To this he lived and to this he taught; and I find it at the very core of all our debt to his life and teaching.

'I remember vividly the day when I first went up to the Italian classroom. It was full of students and full of laughter; and he laughed with them. That was part of his secret. Then he said something so astonishing, so amazing, I have never forgotten it. It struck even the students silent with blank astonishment. He said: "Enjoy learning! That is what you come here for. That is why you learn—to be happy, to enjoy it." It was like something out of a mediaeval tale, beautiful but forgotten. Learning was for examinations, for class tickets, for degrees, for good jobs. But for pleasure? That was an amazing suggestion; but those of us who went to his lectures found it literally true. Whether he spoke on Aristotle and Aquinas, on his old master Carducci, or on Comparative Literature, finding parallels in Milton and Dante, in Petrarch and Shelley, it was all equally alive and enjoyable. It is easily true to say that I learnt more of English literature in the Italian class than in any other.

'The Principal of Perugia University referred to Professor Grillo as "un amico sincero e un collaboratore autorevole", who sent some of his Scottish students every summer to the Royal University for Foreigners there. I was one of those who added this supreme debt: that I owe him Italy. To say what Italy can mean to one is a hopeless task even for a poet. To those of us who came from the grey city in the grey land outside the Roman walls, it was like the golden land of dreams, that land of sunshine and music, of love and light and beauty. It was coming home to the heart and homeland of the Christian civilisation of Europe in which we had all to some extent grown up, and to a people who had an inborn grace of living, a courtesy of the soul that was like the flower of that culture.

'When I went to Italy in 1935, the shadow of Fascism already deterred people, but the Professor used

INTRODUCTION

to say: "Never mind politics—it is people who are important, not politics. Go and meet the people, that's all!" At the time we thought perhaps that was rather an evasion; but now I see it was profound, and I hope the sanity of its simplicity may yet prevail. I found that politics came very little into my stay in Italy, but people a great deal. Although I may perhaps never see Italy again it is so deep in my heart, and so much a background of my thinking and dreaming that it is part of my life for ever. A treasure I hope in some part at least to hand on to my children, trusting they will help to keep up the bridges the Professor laboured to build between Scotland and Italy.

'I stand here as one witness for a host to say the one thing that matters from any student to any teacher: He taught us the Truth. Stone and marble will crumble away; but if a man's work is good it will outlast them. As Dante's *Dream* endures forever may the Professor's vision so endure. As he was our guide, I salute him with Dante's words to his guide in Eternal Truth:

> Non è l'affezion mia tanto profonda,
>   che basti a render voi grazia per grazia;
>   ma quei che vede e puote a ciò risponda.

CULTURAL RELATIONS BETWEEN GREAT BRITAIN AND ITALY

CULTURAL RELATIONS BETWEEN GREAT BRITAIN AND ITALY

It has been asserted that, except for those who are to be specialists, it is more important to know about European civilisation than about the Solar System. If I had my way in the teaching of English literature I would insist that all students start with a general outline of European literature; for it is literature to an even greater extent than the arts that enables us to understand each other's minds, and it is essential that the student should know where its headquarters were situated in each successive period. When Dante is mentioned in connection with Milton, Petrarch with the revival of European lyrical poetry, Boccaccio with Chaucer, Ariosto and Tasso with Spenser, Vida with Pope and Dryden, Mazzini with Carlyle, Croce with contemporary literary criticism, the student ought to be able to assign to all of them their places in the evolution of European literature, and, at the same time, to conceive aright the relation of each to the literary movements in his own particular country.

Comparative studies are not a new departure: all scientific studies are essentially international, and it is only through comparative studies that we obtain the best results in every branch of positive science. The study of Comparative Literature has not yet been formally introduced into all our universities though its importance is widely recognised, but in recent years a movement has been inaugurated for its encouragement, and the history of literature once local and national is becoming European and international. The relations of the various literatures to each other, their actions and reactions, the moral and aesthetic influences that derive from the reciprocal exchange of ideas, all constitute an almost new subject of study which should be of increasing interest to both students and critics, containing as it does the germ of a new method in literary history.

It may be objected that the comparative study of literary works is no novelty, but merely a continuation of ancient criticism. The comparison of Virgil to Homer, Cicero to Demosthenes, Terence to Menander; the debt of Latin authors to the Greeks; the search for the foreign sources from which Plautus derived the material for his comedies, Horace the secrets of his poetic art, and Seneca the plots of his tragedies—these commonplaces of literary history were familiar to ancient criticism. Yet this criticism was never raised to a rigorous scientific method for various reasons, amongst which were the small number of literatures possessed by the ancients, the lack of a critical and historical point of view and the essential dependence of Roman art upon the Greek, whose supremacy remained ever unchallenged in Rome and whose originality was held to be incontestable.

Comparative criticism of artistic works is quite modern. It was the Latin Renaissance, followed by the Greek, that laid the foundation of the comparative method in the modern world, since it was between these two Renaissance periods that nationalities emerged in Europe in the form of distinct groups clearly differentiated by their ethnic origins and their institutions. This transformation of the political state of Europe is of great importance for a true conception of its literary history. The relative unity of thought, which in the Middle Ages had been imposed by the Church, the Empire and the Latin language, began to disintegrate, giving place to new ideas, governments and idioms. Hence also a separation of the literary material; for, while in the Middle Ages the epic, philosophic and historical material was a field common to all peoples, now it was divided, and each nation claimed its share of the conquered spoils in order to appropriate it and affix its own imprint upon it.

Dante marks the beginning of our comparative science by stating in his work, *De Vulgari Eloquentia*, the problem of the nature of languages. He wrote the first monograph dedicated to modern linguistic science. Such was the origin of comparative philology which with the Renaissance was applied to profane texts, and with the Reformation to sacred texts. From this time onwards we may observe the awakening in France, England, Germany and Spain of a lively curiosity regarding anything foreign, especially Italian. All classical antiquity was studied by critics and poets through the medium of Italy. The influence of Italian literature upon the critical and poetic work of the Pléiade Française is very considerable, as it also is on the products of the Elizabethan Age. Luther himself found in Italy a great part of the polemic material for his religious reforms in Germany. Monnier rightly asserted that the German reformer only utilised the ideas and arguments then current in Italy, superimposing on them his doctrine of justification by faith.

Literatures and nations resemble human personalities in that they do not become great in isolation. The study of a living organism is largely that of its relations to its neighbours—inevitable influences and complicated relationships. There is no literature, no writer, no individual whatsoever of whom we might say that his history is confined within the limits of his own country. Modern literatures are a lengthy continuation of the Greek and Latin. Part of the greatness, or at least the glory, of Aristotle is thus due to curious and unexpected good fortune. It is easy to demonstrate that the influence exercised throughout the centuries upon the development of tragedy by the works of Seneca is of vital interest to us. Many ponderous tomes have been produced on the action of Plautus on modern literatures; and, coming nearer our own times, it is incontestable that the history of Petrarchism is of equal interest to Italy, France, England and Spain. The last, and not the least important, chapter to be written on Petrarch will be one characteristic of European literature. The same might be said of Dante, Ariosto, Machiavelli, Tasso, etc.

Voltaire, though never practising the comparative method in his criticism, formulated its principle when he wrote: 'Presque tout est imitation. . . . Il en est des livres comme du feu de nos foyers; on va prendre ce feu chez son voisin, on l'allume chez soi, on le communique à d'autres, et il appartient à tous.' Throughout the history of modern literatures the loans and exchanges for which one is indebted to another should be investigated by the critics. Imitations of Boccaccio can be reckoned by the hundred in every modern language. No one can deny that his works influenced in the highest degree English literature through Chaucer, Shakespeare Dryden, Keats; French through La Fontaine; and German through Hans Sachs, the shoemaker poet of Nuremberg. The greatest European writers have been permeated by foreign influences. The works of Chaucer, Spenser, Shakespeare, Molière and Milton are full of Italian inspiration; English dramatists were indebted for most of their plots to Italian *novellieri*; Corneille owed much to Spain, Rousseau to Germany, Voltaire and Diderot to England.

The literary relations between Italy and Britain are indeed of great interest to the historian, the archaeologist, the artist, the theologian, the poet, the law-giver and, not least, to the man of letters. They may even interest the ordinary tourist when he realises that the Italian universities and academies of Padua, Milan, Pavia, Bologna and Rome were the schools which the scholars of his country frequented in order to gain learning and enlightenment. The whole of Italy is for the tourist a land worthy of loving pilgrimage. In Florence are the remains of Elizabeth Browning, Clough and Landor; in the English cemetery in Rome Keats was buried. Beside the urn enclosing Shelley's ashes, a few steps from the pyramid of Caius Sestius, a noble poet of modern Italy, Giosuè Carducci, sought inspiration:

> 'Fremono freschi i pini per l'aura grande di Roma.
> Tu dove sei poeta del liberato mondo?'

Thus the singer of the Third Italy condensed into two sculptured lines the aspirations of Shelley and, surmounting the melancholy contemplation of the present, took his flight to the purer heavens of immortal ideas through which flashed the radiant vision of a future era of peace and justice.

At Leghorn was buried the Scottish novelist, Tobias Smollett, the celebrated author of *Humphry Clinker*. In Venice the traveller finds the palace where Robert Browning lived and died; in Florence the homes of many English poets. Pisa will remind him of Leigh Hunt's life and sorrows, Spezia and the Tyrrhenian coast of the places where the ill-starred Shelley sought and found his inspiration. Ravenna is memorable for its hospitality to Byron who never tired of singing:

> 'Fair Italy . . .
> Thy very weeds are beautiful, thy waste
> More rich than other climes' fertility.'

Verona, Padua and Milan recall many a lovely scene in Shakespeare's most famous plays; Vallombrosa with its surrounding hills is immortalised in Milton's *Paradise Lost*. The modern pilgrim experiences a thrill of joy on reading the inscription engraved in recent times on the young Puritan's residence:

AN OUTLINE OF CULTURAL RELATIONS

NEL 1638
QUI DIMORÒ IL SOMMO POETA INGLESE
JOHN MILTON
STUDIOSO DEI NOSTRI CLASSICI
DEVOTO ALLA NOSTRA CIVILTÀ
INNAMORATO DI QUESTA FORESTA
E DI QUESTO CIELO

Lucca recalls Ruskin's walks on the cyclopean walls, Genoa the embassies of Chaucer, Naples the invectives of Gladstone and the glorious band of English volunteers who landed there with Garibaldi, the hero of our Risorgimento. Are not all these worthy of great and reverent interest?

In the cultural relations between Britain and Italy we must distinguish five great periods:

    I. From the second century B.C. to the Fall of the Roman Empire.
   II. From the end of the fifth century till the middle of the fourteenth.
  III. From Chaucer till the reign of King Henry VIII.
  IV. From Henry VIII to the death of Milton.
   V. From the beginning of the eighteenth century to our own times.

The First Period

Professor Bury has produced much evidence in support of his theory that the Roman occupation of this country lasted until the middle of the fifth century.

AN OUTLINE OF CULTURAL RELATIONS

The question is chiefly of academic interest but it is an indisputable fact that Roman influences prevailed for at least 450 years. In the process of evolution this is an almost negligible period of time but in the life of a nation it can be of very considerable importance. When we reflect that less than four centuries separate us from the age of Shakespeare, it seems hardly surprising that the Romans should have left indelible traces on every aspect of our civilisation—language, art, local government, religion. 'The great Roman roads still march, with the masterful, indivertible directness of the legions that built them, across the face of the land; and the baths built by these Roman invaders witness yet to a standard of personal cleanliness which we have hardly recaptured in 2,000 years.'

To-day in many British universities there are chairs and lectureships founded to promote the study of Roman influences in Britain; while many men of profound learning like Professor Bury, Bertram Windle, Arthur Weigall and George MacDonald, the numismatist, have spared neither time nor labour to contribute to the enlightenment of the modern world regarding the importance of the Roman occupation of Britain. Prodigious works of excavation and research have been undertaken in many counties of England and Scotland to uncover the remains of our civilisation and assess our relationship with the people of these regions. Remnants of colossal walls and monuments have been found in Bath, Lincoln, York, Bearsden, Falkirk and other places. Villas, temples, baths, mosaics, fountains and coins have during recent years come to light. In rural districts unusually wide furrows still testify to the agricultural methods introduced by the Romans.

But it was not merely material benefits that this amazing race of conquerors bestowed upon the lands of their occupation. The people of Britain received an equally enduring and even more vital inheritance of a less tangible kind. Sir Arthur Quiller-Couch in one of his lectures at Cambridge said: 'I see that this nation of ours, when it seeks back to what alone can inspire and glorify, seeks back, not to any supposed native North, but South to the Middle Sea of our civilisation, and steadily to Italy, which we understand far more easily than France. ... I hasard,' he continues, 'that the most important thing in our blood is that purple drop of the Imperial murex we derive from Rome.'

King George V himself in a public speech acknowledged the magnitude of his country's debt to Italy. 'In a world where all men are each other's debtors the Western World's debt to Italy begins at each nation's birth, since it was from Italy, old in unconquerable youth, that they received the first framing of their laws, life and arts. And the long centuries of unbroken peace between us make Britain and her sons not least of Italy's debtors in civilisation. ... I am happy to think how, alike for Italy and Great Britain, that friendship, deep-rooted in the rich soil of European history, has become a tradition and inspiration. We in these islands are ever mindful of the many ties uniting us to Italy. The influence of Italian genius is apparent in all our arts—in architecture, painting and music; while upon literature that influence was exerted at its earliest and most impressionable age.'

Britain was not merely a nation subjected for a few centuries to the dominion of Rome; it was, Weigall points out, 'as Roman as any other part of the Empire'. Some writers have sought to draw a comparison between the organisation of the Roman Empire and that of the British; but there is one fundamental difference which has often been overlooked—the Romans first conquered and then gave their civilisation, customs, laws and language to a great number of nations, whose elements then, regardless of origin, religion or language, were completely absorbed by the Empire. Thus the Roman people, like the inhabitants of the U.S.A. in our own time, became ever-increasingly a mixture of races.

The Emperor Trajan and Seneca, for example, were Spaniards, the Emperor Severus an African, Virgil a Celt and St. Paul a Jew of Tarsus, but each was entitled to proclaim himself 'Civis Romanus'. In this respect the analogy drawn between the two empires is false; because, though the people of Britain during the Roman occupation were truly Roman, a Canadian, Australian or African has never been entirely British. In the Roman Empire no frontiers divided one race from another and, just as the English, Welsh and Scots are now British, in those days the inhabitants of Britain were as Roman as the Italians themselves.

Rome in fact was not a nation, it was an institution like the Catholic Church, which recognises no barriers of nationality. A tombstone has been found at Newcastle of a Syrian from the city of Palmyra, beyond

Damascus, who had married a British woman and settled in the north of England. In North Africa, on the other hand, an inscription on another tombstone tells of a centurion, British and with a British wife, who had made his home in Mesopotamia. The Syrian and the Briton were alike 'Romans'.

When Julius Caesar invaded Britain his army included cavalry from Gaul, slingers from the Balearic Islands, Numidian archers, Greek and Oriental infantry, while the army of occupation during its long stay in this country was recruited from more than a dozen different nations, all without discrimination Roman. Similarly British-born Romans were sent to all parts of the Empire. What applied to the army was equally true of other professions and trades. All the important centres of Britain in those days were full of administrators, merchants, financiers, artisans, agriculturists from every Roman province. Many of these married British women who, in their turn, lived and dressed in the Roman fashion, spoke the Latin tongue, worshipped in the temples and lived in luxurious villas with baths, central heating and other amenities. It must be borne in mind that it was no brief occupation but a complete Romanisation of the country, whose influence was distinctly felt in every department of civil life.

Second Period

The second period reveals the glories of mediaeval Italy and its potent effect upon the spirit of religion in England. Christianity had been introduced by the legionaries and by Italian missionaries and ecclesiastics, who from the third and fourth centuries occupied prominent posts in the dioceses of Norfolk, Suffolk, Lincoln, London and Worcester. During the twelfth and thirteenth centuries the last mentioned city had four consecutive Italian bishops, who presented it with many valuable MSS., some of which—the MSS. containing, for example, the whole of the Justinian Code—are still shown with pride in the library of the Cathedral. Nor should it be forgotten that some of the greatest Archbishops of Canterbury, like St. Augustine, Lanfranc and Anselm, were Italians or, like Becket, educated in Italy.

Even before the Saxon conquest we find an extraordinary number of English, Scottish and Irish pilgrims in Italy. In the fifth and sixth centuries many of the masters of the great Italian schools, especially those of Pavia, Vercelli and Bologna were English or Scots. In the seventh century a Richard of England, variously described as a king, prince or nobleman, set out for Rome in company with his two sons and his daughter. On the way he fell ill and died at Lucca, where he was buried in the Church of S. Frediano. He is still venerated in that city and is numbered among the Saints of the Church because of the pious errand on which he was engaged at the time of his death. The Roman Breviary describes him as a Prince of the West, and he was depicted as a pilgrim with the Cross on his breast and the Crown at his feet. His sons afterwards continued the journey to Rome, Naples and Capua, and then stopped for a time at Monte Cassino.

AN OUTLINE OF CULTURAL RELATIONS

St. Columbanus, whose persuasive preaching converted King Agilulf, husband of the devout Theodolinda, was given by his royal protector a piece of land on the slopes of the Apennines between Milan and Genoa. There he restored a ruined church and founded the celebrated monastery of Bobbio, which became the most renowned and intellectual of its time in northern Italy and a stronghold of orthodoxy. The abbey church contains the altar which he used and his tomb ornamented with beautiful Celtic interlacing. In the ninth century we find in Fiesole Bishop Donatus and Archdeacon Andrew of Scotland, whose sister, St. Bride, after his death lived in a cave in the neighbourhood and was associated with the Benedictine Order. A church was built over her tomb and she is still venerated in Fiesole.

In the eighth century King Ina had founded in Rome a hospice for pilgrims. The guests received there were of two kinds: *nobiles et pauperes*. The former contributed towards the maintenance of the hospice, the latter were admitted '*gratis et amore*'. A list compiled in the sixteenth century describes the social position of the visitors, many of whom were clergy, teachers, ambassadors and princes. The ambassadors of King Henry VII, Edward Scot and John Alen, lived there during the time of their residence in Rome. Amongst the poorer guests we find students, sailors and peasants who, from Ireland, Scotland and England were attracted to Italy by the glory of the Eternal City and a desire to visit the tombs of the Apostles. We may assume that a part of this, as of similar hostels, was reserved for women; for we find among the list of visitors names of prominent English ladies chiefly from London, Norfolk and Suffolk. If to all these we add the innumerable company of British friars and Bishops who from the early Middle Ages had been educated in the seminaries and schools of Italy, and who then brought back to their native land the encyclopaedic learning of the Italian colleges we shall have some idea of the powerful influence Italian religious thought exercised in the British Isles.

The majority of English schools were, both before and after A.D. 1000, founded by Italian Popes and Bishops to encourage the study of literature and the arts among those students who were too poor to pursue their studies in France or Italy. The English universities themselves were founded later in the same manner to familiarise English students with the study of law and theology. The greatest and most celebrated of Scottish schools were also of Italian origin. The Universities of St. Andrews, Glasgow and Aberdeen were not only founded by Italian Popes but still possess the constitution of the Italian universities of the Renaissance.

This love of culture and the fine arts was greatly encouraged in the thirteenth century by the advent of the Franciscans whose monasteries, assuming the monopoly of educational and charitable institutions, soon became famous. A study of Franciscan influences in England might alone fill several volumes. The spirit of English literature was completely transformed by these friars, who provided some of the most outstanding representatives of British learning in the thirteenth and fourteenth centuries, amongst them Bishop Grosseteste of Lincoln, Roger Bacon, John Langland and Richard of Bury, learned in Latin, Greek and Hebrew, the author of the Filobiblion and of the first Greek and Hebrew grammars designed for students in this country. He was twice in Rome as an ambassador to Pope John XXII, who appointed him a Papal Chaplain. At Avignon in 1330 he met Petrarch, who has left a brief account of their intercourse.

Third Period

The third period of Anglo-Italian literary relations begins with Chaucer who, on his three visits to Italy, found there inspiration for many of his inimitable works, some of which, like *Troilus and Cressida*, *The Knightes Tale*, *The Clerkes Tale*, *The Legend of Good Women*, etc., are no more than a translation and rehandling of Italian works, in particular the *Filostrato*, *Teseide*, *Donne Illustri* and *Decamerone* of Boccaccio. Besides these he introduced many passages from Dante, Petrarch and the minor poets of the fourteenth century into his *Canterbury Tales*, which, in their turn, were translated in masterly fashion into Italian by Chiarini, the friend of Carducci.

Chaucer was followed by John Lydgate, whose volume *The Fall of Princes* is a translation of Boccaccio's work on *Illustrious Men*; by Gower and by the Scottish Chaucerians, who included men like William Dunbar, a Franciscan friar, Robert Henryson, the fabulist, and Sir David Lindsay, whose *Dream* in which the poet journeys under the guidance of Dame Remembrance from earth to hell, thence to high heaven is reminiscent of Dante's *Divine Comedy*.

At this period too Italian influence gave a great impetus to the study of law and the humanities in England. These studies were encouraged in the universities and courts, which were specially favourable to the works of our masters. Italian poets were always sure of a cordial welcome; while humanists, lecturers and rhetoricians were greatly in demand for the teaching of Greek, Latin and Italian in schools and colleges.

From Harrison's *Description of England* we learn that Cambridge University was so destitute of Latinists that it had to procure the services of an Italian for the composition of orations and epistles. In those days the Orator was the most conspicuous member of the academic body, and some modern universities have retained the post of Public Orator, which has been given to men eminent in arts or letters as, for example, Ruskin, Arnold, Raleigh, etc.

Pietro Carmeliano of Brescia was appointed Court Poet, Secretary and Chaplain by Henry VII, who granted him handsome emoluments. The last poem he wrote was on the occasion of the death of James IV of Scotland at the Battle of Flodden. Adriano di Castello belongs to the same category. After being Apostolic Nuncio to Scotland he became Collector of St. Peter in England, was naturalised and then sent by Henry VII as Ambassador to the Court of Pope Alexander VI. In 1488 we find at Oxford a certain Cornelio Vitelli, who had come to give 'that barbarous university' some idea of classical literature. Italian humanists like Cardinal Enea Piccolomini and the students of the celebrated Guarino Veronese visited England in search of MSS. and some believe that even Dante and Petrarch were included among these research workers. It is certain, however, that Poggio Bracciolini visited London, Canterbury and York but was disappointed at finding little of interest there. 'Many of the monastic libraries', he wrote, 'are full of trash.'

The men of learning, poets and artists at the Court of Duke Humphrey of Gloucester were Italians. Since not only princes but nobles and clergy adopted the practice of employing Italians for educational purposes, a large number of our humanists occupied positions of importance in England. Girolamo Gigli, canon, bishop and orator of Henry VIII, went to Rome to further the cause of the royal divorce. Polidoro Virgilio, friend of the same king, became first Historiographer of England, and was confronted with the task of compiling a history of the country from records which were confused and dispersed. Besides the musicians, fencing masters, actors and court jesters, the physicians of the period were also sons of Italy.

Towards the end of the fifteenth century Grocyn, fresh from the teaching of Politian in Florence, arrived to teach Greek in Exeter College, Oxford, where he was soon followed by Colet and by Linacre who, on leaving Italy, had erected a monument to commemorate his residence there. These are some of the best known of that multitude of English students who visited Italy and remained to attend lectures from our most famous teachers—Politian, Guarino Veronese, Filelfo and Vittorino da Feltre.

With the Reformation ecclesiastical relations between the two countries increased rather than diminished. The defenders of King Henry VIII were lawyers of the University of Padua, where the number of English and Scottish students was so large that they organised themselves into two special guilds: the Scottish Nation and the English Nation, whose members caused to be engraved on a marble tablet in the public square of the city the famous inscription 'Sancta Mater Studiorum'.

After the death of Queen Mary pious English Catholics fled to Italy, forming in many cities an important nucleus for the revival of religious ideas. John Clerk of Oxford lived for many years in Italy, writing treatises on theological questions in both Latin and Italian, and became so fascinated by the literature of Italy that he came to prefer it to either the Latin or the Greek. William Lilly, the grammarian, and his son George, settled in Rome, where they became famous for their erudition. Not only was the poet Heywood attracted to Italy, but his brother Ellis became a Jesuit, was appointed secretary to a cardinal and wrote in Italian two dialogues on love, inspired by the neoplatonic doctrines of the Italian Renaissance. In Italy too, lived Sir Edward Carne, who had gone there to defend King Henry VIII, when the latter was summoned to appear in person. It was rumoured that he was held a prisoner, but the fact is that his stay was entirely voluntary and his detention by the Pope merely an excuse to enable him retain his property in England.

AN OUTLINE OF CULTURAL RELATIONS

The most outstanding representative of Anglo-Catholic culture to be found in Italy was Cardinal Reginald Pole, who maintained unblemished the dignity of his country. After studying at Oxford under Linacre and Latimer (both former students of the poet Politian) he proceeded to the University of Padua, which he called 'Helladis Hellas'. There he became leader of the English colony and gathered around him a band of scholars and poets. He is one of the commanding figures of the age but, in spite of his interest in humanism, his chief motive was the restoration of the supremacy of Rome in England. He made it abundantly clear to the English people that it was possible to be a humanist, to live in Italy and yet remain unaffected by the supposed vices prevalent there. Exercising as he did considerable influence he was an important link between the two countries. Englishmen saw in him the authority and grandeur of Rome, Italians the piety and austerity of England. At the time when Ascham was inveighing against the English aristocracy's habit of travelling in Italy, Pole and his friends published a manifesto declaring that one could be a humanist, poet and philosopher and live in Italy with honour and without contamination.

In 1575 Pope Gregory XIII founded in Rome an English college, to which was subsequently added a hospital, under the patronage of a cardinal. Over 350 English students were admitted there annually to the priesthood, many of them returning to England to devote themselves to the conversion of their brethren. Before leaving Rome they went to kiss the Pope's feet and receive money for their travelling expenses. A record has been preserved of the fate of many of these missionary martyrs; and students of ecclesiastical history will find a full account of their sufferings in Taunton's great work on the subject. It is sufficient to say here that the American, English, Scottish and Irish colleges which now exist in Rome are a continuation of those established in the Middle Ages.

Visits to Italian university cities had become so common that the Puritans considered it necessary to make a public protest. Characteristic of the accusations made against these students who rebelled at the uncouth habits of their homeland are the words of the preacher who asserted that all these youths brought back from abroad were 'a naughty conscience, a weak stomach and an empty purse'. In the England of those days manners and customs were still primitive; at meals servants brought 'basins and ewers to lave the dainty hands' which had been used in eating, and it was probably one of these young travellers who introduced the fork at Court. Such was the amazement caused by the sight of this implement that it earned for him the title of 'Forcifer'. In Coryat's account of his travels we read: 'I observed a custom in all those Italian cities and towns through which I passed, that is not used in any other country that I saw in my travels, neither do I think that any other nation of Christendom doth use it but only Italy. The Italian and also most strangers that are commorant in Italy do always at their meals use a little fork when they cut their meat. For while with their knife which they hold in one hand they cut the meat out of the dish, they fasten their fork which they hold in their other hand upon the same dish...'

Italian modes introduced by the students were fiercely resented by admirers of the old native rusticity, and the novelties were denounced by preachers in the churches and satirists in their verses. In 1512 Masques were introduced into England. Edward Hull tells us that at Epiphany the King himself took part in them along with his young courtiers disguised in the Italian fashion. Jousts and tournaments were also revived at Court. Sir Christopher Hatton, a patron of arts and letters and an enthusiastic admirer of Italian literature, played a leading part in their revival. The best artists of the time were entrusted with the decorations, and our musicians with their sweet melodies added to the enjoyment of the youthful high-spirited crowds.

Men of intelligence and good taste, following the example of our academies, began to turn their attention to the English language, which they felt to be rough and barbarous, and to make it their duty to purify it and enrich it by the addition of words of foreign origin. Thousands of Italian words—especially those connected with the fine arts, law, music, religion, science, literature and medicine—soon came to be assimilated. Besides the traces to be found in Henryson, Dunbar and Douglas, Italian influences made themselves felt before the advent of Wyatt and Surrey in works by Stephen Hawes, the *Pastime of Pleasure* and the *Example of Virtue*, and in those of the poet Skelton, who was responsible for introducing into this country the type of verse known in Italy as 'macaronic'. This was very popular in fifteenth-century Tuscany, and its chief exponent was Folengo whose works, admired and imitated by Rabelais, appeared in 1521.

All this serves to show that in the period between Chaucer and Wyatt and Surrey literary relations between Britain and Italy remained active and uninterrupted. Moreover, the same phenomenon is apparent in both countries. Just as in Italy after Petrarch and Boccaccio up till the time of Lorenzo de'Medici, Pulci, Politian and Boiardo our literature was abandoned by men of learning in favour of a study of the classics, so in England for the same reason there are no great writers in the popular tongue from Chaucer until Wyatt and Surrey.

The Reformation has been considered as a counterpart of the Renaissance but the ethical and religious influences of Italy have not been sufficiently appreciated. The elucidation of the Holy Scriptures together with the severe aspect of our national life and the religious fervour of Savonarola have been obscured by the iniquities of a few Spaniards—the Borgias. Little or no credit has been given to the effects of Italian thought and criticism on Linacre, Latimer, Grocyn, Colet and Erasmus; and of the works of Dante, Marsilius of Padua, Petrarch, St. Catherine of Siena, Valla, Politian and of the Popes Nicholas V, founder of the University of Glasgow, and Pius II who wrote much about Scotland.

The English reformers themselves made use of the works of the Italian 'rebels' in various phases of their religious reformation. Pietro Martire Vermigli, the son of one of Savonarola's disciples, after studying for eight years in Padua, came to England on the invitation of Cranmer and became Professor of Divinity at Oxford and an ardent champion of the Reformation. Many of the collaborators of John Knox in Scotland came from Italian universities and Friar Ochimo of the Capuchin Order, the popular Elizabethan preacher, founded an Italian Church in London and produced many literary works, one of which—*Tragedy*—containing violent accusations against the Catholic Church, was the subject of a study by Dr. Garnett, who found in it passages parallel to parts of Milton's *Paradise Lost*. To such Italians is due the fact that the Anglican Church so largely retained the organisation of the Church of Rome. Angelo Florio, father of the celebrated John Florio, the friend of Shakespeare and translator of Montaigne, was another Italian reformer who settled in London; whilst Jacopo Aconzio from Siena, author of a volume entitled *Satan's Stratagems*, also supported the cause of the English Reformation. In addition to this, translations of Italian religious literature appropriate to the mentality and spirit of the English were widely circulated for the edification of the masses of the people.

Nor should the Italian influence at this period upon English commerce be overlooked. The presence in London, Bristol and Southampton of many educated Italians of great business ability and superior methods could not fail to stimulate local industries and commercial undertakings. The Mediterranean was at that time the centre of the Old World's commercial life; and companies of merchants from Florence, Siena, Pisa, Umbria, Venice and Lombardy had the monopoly of

AN OUTLINE OF CULTURAL RELATIONS

European trade fairs and markets. As early as the eleventh century many of them had settled in London, choosing as the centre of their commercial activities a street in the heart of the city, whose name—Lombard Street—still recalls those ventures. Many words of Italian origin were soon introduced into English commercial phraseology e.g. debtor, creditor, cash, bank, journal, company, florin, etc.

The 'Mercatores Tusciae' were held in high repute and the Ubaldini, heads of a Florentine company, were appointed governors of Windsor Castle. These merchants were followed by the celebrated bankers, the Bardi, Peruzzi, Frescobaldi, Guidotti, Pallavicini, Medici and Chigi, to whom we owe the organisation of our modern system of banking. In times of financial embarrassment, kings and princes of England were obliged to obtain loans from them; while these Italian bankers were often entrusted with the administration of the sovereign's patrimony, local taxation and the control of imports and exports.

King John, father of Isabella, wife of the Emperor Frederick II of Sicily, Henry II, Edwards I, II, III and IV, Henry VII, Henry VIII and even Cromwell all had recourse to these bankers, to whom was also entrusted the construction of the port of Southampton, which was destined to become the focus of Anglo-Italian trade. It is of interest to recall that Chaucer himself was sent at least thrice to Italy in order to negotiate trade agreements between Italian cities and his native land, and how English literature has been enriched by the results of these journeys.

Frequently Italian business men were reduced to extreme poverty on account of the unredeemed pledges of English kings and princes. The Bardi company suffered disaster as a result of lending large sums to Prince Henry, son of Henry II; the Leopardis sacrificed a good part of their capital to liberate a Lord Derby from a debtors' prison in Paris, while the firm of Bardi and Peruzzi was reduced to bankruptcy by lending huge sums to Edward III, sums which he in his turn had lent for the prosecution of the war against France and could not afterwards repay. The failure of this banking company was for Italy and Europe a great disaster, whose grave consequences were felt by the historian Villani himself, who has handed down the information to us.

Towards the middle of the fourteenth century Venetian galleys began to appear in the port of Southampton, which continued for more than two hundred years to be the outlet for trade with Italy. The Venetians were also of great assistance to the English in their wars against France; in 1340 they conceded to Edward III the use of forty of their ships, which served with distinction throughout the period of hostilities. As an expression of gratitude for their valuable services the King granted to the citizens of Venice all the privileges enjoyed by his own subjects, at the same time inviting the Doge to send his sons to the English Court, and promising to educate and treat them as his own and to confer knighthoods upon them. Venetian ambassadors have left us interesting documents which are important for a study of the history of

English civilisation. From many points of view Venice was then what Britain afterwards became—'a nation of shopkeepers'—and her colonies formed an empire governed by an aristocracy of merchants. England's knowledge of the Orient came to her by way of Italy; and to Venice is due the credit of uniting East and West in a common bond of commerce.

At a later date Italian books of travel and adventure imported in large numbers from Rome, Venice and Florence fired the imagination of the Elizabethans with their tales of treasure and conquest. Italian bankers and merchants had demonstrated to the English people all the possibilities of a commercial life. In the field of exploration and discovery the example of Marco Polo, Columbus, the Cabots and not least Amerigo Vespucci's descriptions of the New World all contributed to foster the love of adventure, of which we detect an echo in so many literary works, especially in the *Utopia* of More, the *Nuova Atlantis* of Bacon and, in more modern times, in Defoe's *Robinson Crusoe* and Stevenson's *Treasure Island*. In the sphere of commerce, as of the arts and sciences, Italy revealed to the world new ideals, new methods, new possibilities; the energy and ardour of our Renaissance are reflected not only in the works of poets and artists, but just as clearly in the mercantile history of Britain.

Fourth Period

In this glorious period of English literature the Italian Renaissance was made known to the Elizabethans by hundreds of translators, who included nearly every notable writer of the age. Shakespeare's name does not appear in this long list of translators, but all must recognise him as the soul of romantic drama; and English romantic drama not only derived from Italian literature four-fifths of its plots, ideas and general inspiration, but borrowed from Italian drama much of its technique—chorus, echo, play within a play, dumb show, ghosts of great men, mechanical stage apparatus and all the physical horrors which aroused in the audience feelings of awe and terror. Moreover, we must not forget the influence which both the *Commedia dell'Arte* and the *Commedia Erudita* exercised on English tragedy and comedy.

The plots of sixteen Shakespearian plays are to be found in Italian fiction; while others, even the most original, like *Hamlet* and *Macbeth*, contain much of the life, customs and art of Italy. The works translated into English were representative of all the best known Italian writers on every subject. In commerce and discovery Marco Polo, Columbus, the Cabots and Amerigo Vespucci are the last of a long line of navigators who, in the service of the Western nations, undertook voyages to distant and unknown lands in order to enrich their Spanish, Portuguese or English patrons. In the field of history translations of the works of Machiavelli, Guicciardini, Bentivoglio, Segni and Varchi prepared the way for the new school of English historians—Hall, Grafton, Stow, Holinshed. In politics and diplomacy English statesmen like Henry VII, Henry VIII, Thomas Cromwell, Francis Bacon,

Queen Elizabeth, Sir George Fenton, the Earl of Monmouth, etc. followed in the footsteps of our diplomatists. In philosophy the new theories propounded by intrepid spirits like Telesio, Bruno and Campanella, who, having dethroned Aristotle, the idol of the Schools, cast off for ever the fetters of Scholasticism, found ardent supporters among the English. Nor must it be forgotten that it was Elizabethan London and Oxford that accorded freedom of speech to the unhappy Giordano Bruno. In literary criticism the works of Trissino, Vida, Minturno, Poggio, Filelfo, Castelvetro, amongst many writers of the time, gave a great impetus to the rising English school of criticism in which Sidney's *Apology for Poetrie* and Puttenham's *Art of English Poesie* were the forerunners of Pope's *Essay on Criticism* and Shelley's *Defence of Poetry*.

In life and social customs Italy occupied first place with her innumerable publications on the philosophy of good manners. The *Cortegiano* of Castiglione, the *Galateo* of Della Casa, Bembo's *Asolani* and Guazzo's *Book of Polite Conversation* by providing standards of conduct and counsels for the refinement of society and by initiating a more elegant type of literature prepared the way for the Scholar Gentleman of the English Renaissance. When the divine Spenser platonises in his Hymns on Love and Celestial Beauty he is merely reproducing the theories of Cardinal Bembo, the literary dictator of the sixteenth century. The history of Court and social life in England would be incomplete without a reference to those books which contributed to the rise of the new type of nobleman like Surrey and Philip

Sidney. The many references to them and the influence they exerted on the works of the great European writers give them a historical and ethical value for the study of literature and the arts even today in our so-called advanced state of civilisation.

In medicine and astronomy Italian scientists revealed to the world the mysteries of Nature. Harvey brought back from Padua the new theories on the circulation of the blood; and Milton, travelling in Italy at a later date, visited at Arcetri the greatest of all, the unhappy Galileo, blind and in exile for his study of the heavenly bodies.

The delicate forms of the new lyrical poetry, for instance the sonnets of Wyatt, Surrey, Sidney, Spenser and Shakespeare, were permeated by the passionate idealism of the *Vita Nuova* and the *Canzoniere*. With their vivacious and sonorous stanzas Spenser also received from Ariosto and Tasso the richly colourful spirit of Italian descriptive poetry. From the splendid and artistic prose evolved by Machiavelli and Guicciardini Francis Bacon reproduced their cold, calculating philosophy. From the reading of the harmonious verse of Politian, Lorenzo de'Medici, Pulci and Boiardo and from a study of the works of Botticelli, Raphael, Giorgione, Titian, Veronese and Tintoretto men like Greene and Dorset acquired that delightful pictorial quality which shines with such Olympian serenity in Shakespeare's *Venus and Adonis* and *Rape of Lucrece*, and in Marlowe's *Sextiad*. From Italian pastoral poetry, from Politian's *Orfeo*, Tasso's *Aminta*, Guarini's *Pastor Fido*, and from numerous tales with a sylvan setting, poets like Spenser, Fletcher and Allan Ramsay derived the wealth of imagery and delicacy of sentiment which still arouse the admiration of their modern readers. In our fifteenth- and sixteenth-century Platonists—Marsilio Ficino, Pico della Mirandola, Castiglione—English writers found many of those neo-platonic theories so nobly expounded by Spenser, the Elizabethans, seventeenth-century poets like Crashaw, Vaughan, Herbert, Donne and, at a later period, Shelley. Folengo, Boccalini and Berni at the very least helped to interpret to the more sombre English intellect the sunny smile and charm of southern wit.

From the *Novelle*, on which more than three-quarters of English dramatic works in the sixteenth and seventeenth centuries were based, and from the Italian Epicureans of the Renaissance English playwrights learned that *joie de vivre* and stoicism in facing death which are so impressively portrayed by Shakespeare, Marlowe, Beaumont and Fletcher, and even by the 'wild and savage Webster'. But along with the abstract, with Italian modes of thought and poetic forms—sonnet, ottava rima, Spenserian stanza, etc.—the Elizabethans brought back the concrete and personal. Their works are full of reminiscences of Italy: from complete plots taken from the *Novelle* to mere passing allusions to places or customs; from continuous descriptions of theatrical performances to single phrases evoking a glimpse of gardens, palaces, cities, rivers or it may be of actors, musicians and dancers, yet all revealing to the crowds who thronged the Globe or Blackfriars Theatre that marvellous Italy which every Englishman of the period had learned to know at least in spirit and to love.

Of all foreign influences which contributed to the formation of taste and thought in the England of the glorious Elizabethan epoch the Italian was undoubtedly the most conspicuous and far-reaching; and the fashion of imitating things Italian did not cease with the Renaissance but continued to make itself felt notably in the music, lyrical poetry and sciences of the seventeenth century. Hallam, commenting upon the harmonious sweetness of much of the poetry in this period, is in entire agreement with those critics who attribute this quality to the growing love of music. And this is perfectly true because the harmony of this new poetic inspiration is but the prelude to the effects our divine melodies were to have in arousing Europe from a state of torpor.

In the times of the Stuarts we find other new characteristics. All the English poets seem fascinated by the ideas and conceits of our *Secentismo*. Not even the Puritan Marvell could escape from this tendency, which continued in vogue until the days of Dryden and Pope. Some of Crashaw's poems are translations and imitations of Marini, and several of the liveliest of Herrick's lyrics (e.g. *To live merrily, and to trust to Good Verses*) are free reproductions of the sentiments expressed by our poets. Here we must observe that, although in his early days Marvell came under the spell of the graceful forms and imagery of the Italian Renaissance, in later life he rejected both the forms and spirit of Boccaccio, Ariosto, Marini and the *novellieri* in general and returned to seek inspiration in Dante, Petrarch and the fourteenth-century mystics. In his great poem, *Clorinda and Damon*, a dialogue between the Soul and Pleasure, we seem to detect an echo of Petrarch, especially in the parts where all the most seductive charms fail to beguile the soul of the hero.

Another style of poetry prevalent in the first half of the seventeenth century and in part adopted by Donne, Lovelace, Crashaw, Herrick and several others, was that called 'metaphysical' by Dr. Johnson and by others merely 'fantastic'. This began to flourish on the decline of the Elizabethan Age, at the time when some poets were writing under the influence of Euphuism, which had already begun to manifest itself in Spenser, Sidney, Shakespeare and some of the minor Elizabethans. Through their elaborate metaphors, strange antitheses, far-fetched conceits, pompous descriptions and a tendency to sacrifice clarity of thought to artifice of expression Donne and Herrick are in the direct line of descent of our poets of the decadent school whose style, with its well-known defects of affectation, goes by the name of secentism. This type of poetry was developed in England under the influence of Marini who, in Italy, France and Spain was the fashionable poet of the day. Donne, Crashaw and Herbert were 'marinists', while Herrick proclaimed him the poet of the new generation and Carew greeted him as the inspirer of the Muses.

The Italian genius of the Renaissance found its noblest expression in the fine arts. It was only natural that Italian artists should travel through the various countries of Europe reawakening the cult of art. It is a fact worthy of notice, however, that not one of our greatest artists visited Britain in the sixteenth century, though many were to be found at the Court of Charles V, and Francis I was the patron of both Leonardo and Benvenuto Cellini. Pietro Torrigiano is the best known of those who came to seek their fortune in England. The execution of the monument in Henry VII's Chapel, Westminster Abbey, was entrusted to him. Besides this he undertook upon the King's commission several statues in marble and bronze and also the famous tomb of Dr. Young, Master of the Rolls, now in the Museum of the Record Office in London, which is an excellent example of the imaginative ornamentation of the Tuscan School. Another important work of his was the tomb of Henry VII and his Queen, also in Westminster Abbey. Although this is not typically Tuscan in style, it yet exhibits the technique of that school in the bronze figures, medallions on the base and many other details. But Torrigiano's masterpiece in England was the tomb of Margaret of Richmond, one of the most beautiful monuments the Abbey possesses. Henry VIII wanted him to undertake his tomb and that of Queen Katherine, but this project had to be abandoned owing to the artist's departure for Spain.

Amongst other Italian artists employed by Henry VII we may mention the architect Mazzoni and the painters Volpe, Toto and Cavallari, as well as the miniaturist Alice Carmeliana. Toto is equally renowned as an architect and as a designer of masks, but was one of the best of the Italian painters who came to England. He had studied under Ghirlandaio and, after being introduced at Court by Torrigiano, was appointed Sergeant Painter there. Many of his frescoes are still to be seen in Cardinal Wolsey's apartments at Hampton Court, where, finding time amidst the cares of State to encourage the cult of art and letters, the Cardinal also gave employment to Giovanni da Maiano, who was later entrusted with the execution of his patron's tomb, which was to be magnificent and worthy of the taste of a great Prince of the Church. Da Maiano worked at it for five years, but after the Cardinal's death the unfinished work was sent to Windsor, where the marble sarcophagus was afterwards used for the tomb of Nelson and the pedestal utilised in the construction of George III's vault.

Nor was it only to London that the Italian artists came. The brothers Bernardi settled in Chichester and were the first Italian decorators in these parts, while the Duke of Somerset employed Giovanni da Modena and Giovanni da Padua, entrusting to the latter the design of his new town house in the Strand. The influence of these artists was especially felt throughout the southern counties, where small colonies of Italians settled, but traces of their work are to be found in many other places such as Lincoln, Cambridge and Suffolk and in many of the mansions of the English aristocracy. A German traveller spoke of the presence in England in those days of large numbers of Italian architects, sculptors and craftsmen, whose genius was not only utilised in the decoration but also in the actual building of important town and country houses. The example of their industry, their technical ability and the novelty of forms and designs introduced by them were an amazing revelation to British workmen and gave an impetus to local arts and crafts.

In Elizabeth's time. the painters Trezzo, Ubaldini, Primavera and Zuccaro were in England. Trezzo painted the portrait of Queen Mary, Zuccaro that of Elizabeth, while Ubaldini was employed as a miniaturist and illuminator. Elizabethan England, however, on account of the Reformation and the triumph of Puritanism was not ready to receive the message of Italian art; so, notwithstanding all endeavours to acclimatise the fine arts of Italy, England had to wait for the development of her classical architecture till the days of Inigo Jones and Christopher Wren, who, having studied for many years in Italy, brought back to their native land the style of Bramante and Palladio; for painting till the times of Hogarth, Gainsborough, Romney, Reynolds, Rossetti, Millais, etc., and for sculpture till the early nineteenth century and the influence of Canova.

At the end of the English Renaissance much of what was best in Italy in the field of literature and criticism had been transplanted in England, though in a few instances the desired results had not been attained; as, for example, in the case of the fine arts, which had been prevented from taking firm root; but, in general, all that was suitable for the northern land had found its way there; literature, science, social customs and the art of diplomacy were all affected by Italian influences.

AN OUTLINE OF CULTURAL RELATIONS

Perhaps the greatest representative of Italian culture in England during the seventeenth century was Milton, who travelled widely in Italy and even wrote Italian verse in praise of a young lady with whom he had fallen in love. One circumstance early aroused in him an interest in Italy—his most intimate schoolfriend was Carlo Diodati (nephew of the Protestant theologian in Geneva), who exercised a great influence upon the future poet and helped to foster in him a love for our country which was to increase with time and with further study of the classics.

Italian influence, and especially that of Dante, is remarkable in the works of Milton. His own desire was to be an English Tasso, and he was an enthusiast for the theories of neo-classical criticism. His *Samson Agonistes* gives us the impression of a regular classical tragedy, while *Paradise Lost* has all the attributes of a classical Italian poem—its versification even brings to mind that Italy, whose landscape suggested some of the most brilliant descriptive passages in the poem. The episodes of the Paradise of Fools and the Limbus of Vanities are taken from Ariosto. The council of demons and the troops of rebellious angels rising in flight to reach the Council Chamber come from Tasso. So also in *Paradise Regained*, in *Comus*, the Sonnets, *L'Allegro*, *Il Penseroso* and in his prose are to be found clear indications of a study of our literature.

Milton had begun to study Italian before 1632 and his mind, susceptible to impressions made by books, was specially attracted by our poetry. Absorbed in a study of Dante, Petrarch, Ariosto, Tasso and Marini he conceived the desire of visiting Italy to hear for himself the music of our *'dolce favella toscana'*. The fatal gift of beauty which had excited the envy of the barbarians in every age still has, and will always have, the magnetic power of attracting the minds of men. Many are the sources of this fascination. The scholar, artist, archaeologist, poet, lover of scenery, all find in Italy ample satisfaction for their diverse tastes. Though not insensible to all other attractions, Milton felt urged to cross the Alps chiefly by a desire to converse with the poets and men of learning who still kept alive the traditions of the great classical age.

Among his letters of introduction was one from the aged Sir Henry Wotton of Eton College, who lived not far from the poet's home. Wotton, who had been for several years in Italy, impressed upon his young friend the necessity of being discreet especially on religious questions, counselling him to keep 'close thoughts and open countenance'. The times of the Counter-Reformation and the Council of Trent were over and the poet might have dispensed with the advice all the more because, as far as his personal opinions upon the faith and doctrines of the Church were concerned, the new admirer of the glories of Italy was as tenacious in defending them as his opponents were in disputing them.

Milton was able both to speak and write Italian; and he took our poets for his guide and example in the high ideal he set himself of giving to England the Christian Epic, which Tasso had already given to Italy, but which he himself by political events was prevented from beginning until twenty years later. A story was told that when he was a student at Cambridge he fell asleep one day on the grass in the shade of a tree. Two Italian ladies, happening to pass in their carriage, were so entranced by his handsome appearance that they stopped and one of them, leaving the carriage, slipped into his hand a piece of paper on which were two lines from the *Gerusalemme Liberata*. Some fellow-students who had glimpsed this brief idyll related the story to Milton, and, according to the legend, he realised from that day what was to be his poetical mission. But in reality his mission, like his affection for Italy, had a higher and more distant origin. It came to him from that troubled and amazing seventeenth ·century, torn between its love for the heroic and disciplined greatness of antiquity and its audacious curiosity for all that was, or appeared, new. In this period the human intellect prided itself in new experimental sciences, which every day discovered new worlds, whether among the stars in the firmament or the grass in the meadows, and deluded itself into believing that it could storm the citadels of the Infinite. It saw the Church of Rome restored, the Anglican Schism in the land of Shakespeare and Milton, and the Calvinism of John Knox triumphant in Scotland.

In the realm of art the architecture of Imperial Rome was revived with such majestic grandeur in the cathedrals and cloisters of the Catholic Church that foreign architects, especially English and Scottish, having come like Milton on a pilgrimage to Italy, returned to erect their classical domes and colonnades under British skies, just as Milton raised to heaven the melodious verses of his *Paradise Lost*, dreaming still of Petrarch, Ariosto and Tasso. Music was revitalised in Church, Court, theatre and street; and even a Florentine saint—S. Filippo Neri—in his Oratory sought to restore to it, by the purity of his ardour, the joy and glory of being the most direct path leading from man to his Creator. Milton, too, loved this music of ours and on his arrival in Florence, Rome, Naples and Venice he hastened to listen to it. In the cases of Italian books which, at the end of his journey, he despatched to England to await his homecoming were volumes of our music from Palestrina to Vecchi, and from Vecchi to Monteverde.

'Italy, Italy,' exclaimed every scholar in admiration; yet within her own borders men dared to call 'decadent' the century of Galilei, Gravina, Vico, Muratori and Berni. The Italians themselves called it decadent, and immediately, beyond the Alps, the foreigners re-echoed the epithet because, at that precise moment, the national arts of England, France and Spain were finally taking shape, and it was in the foreigners' own interest to discredit the source of their inspiration. Rather was the seventeenth century in Italy a period of passion, faith, life and hope which still lives on in science, art, music and philosophy.

Fifth Period

After the death of Milton, Italian influences remained more or less stationary in England. The lack of fresh vigour on the part of our writers and the attacks of the Puritans had combined to weaken them. The place of Italy was being taken by France and Spain, both of which were enjoying a flourishing period of culture, but both, with new forms and methods, still revealing indirectly the culture and civilisation of Italy. It was the same Italy, transformed and bearing the imprint of France and Spain, whose foster-children were for historical reasons to continue the work begun by her. Italian thought, though less generally apparent than formerly, was still evident in the works of Dryden, Pope, Addison, Goldsmith and Johnson, while our operas added lustre to the London stage. In the eighteenth century the inspiration of Italy had a twofold triumph: by her gift of music and the fine arts she embellished and enlivened the home life of her friends in Britain. In the works of such great artists as Sir Joshua Reynolds (worthily called the Correggio of England), Hogarth, Gainsborough, Turner, Flaxman, Blake and later in those of Rossetti, Millais, Burne-Jones, Watts, etc. Italian influences are clearly manifest.

Here we must mark a slight difference which begins to be noticeable in the attitude of great Englishmen towards Italy. Now there is no lack of generous voices sincerely deploring the tragic conditions of political servitude prevailing in our peninsula. Amongst the noblest of these voices is that of Addison, whose visit to Italy inspired that 'Letter from Italy' to Charles, Lord Halifax, which is the finest poetic effort of the famous editor of the *Spectator*. None can deny the sincerity of the sentiments arising from the striking contrast between the splendours of natural beauty and

Italian art and the chill mists of the north; between the conditions of servitude in Italy and the triumph of liberty in England. What value have these glories of nature and art, concludes the poet, if they are obscured by the dark clouds of tyranny and oppression? These generous words are but the prelude to the intense love and admiration of the nineteenth century. The affection for Italy experienced by Chaucer, Shakespeare and Milton is very different from the sentiment we can trace in more modern writers. The contemporaries of Shakespeare and Milton regard Italy as a great and wonderful museum of works of art and glorious ancient monuments. The later writers love our peninsula, but love the Italians also. For them Italy is a great and noble nation, blessed by nature and worthy of rising again to the highest destiny; and they cannot conceive her apart from her inhabitants. Our aspirations become their aspirations; they rejoice over the victories of Italy and mourn over her defeats, sharing in her joys and sorrows, hopes and disappointments.

In the eighteenth century Italian music, painting, sculpture, architecture and, above all, landscape and politics had many admirers in England; and, as it drew to a close, they once more turned to Italy for inspiration in their Romantic Revival and later for Pre-Raphaelitism and the Oxford Movement. Coleridge, Warton and Gray were the first writers of this period to reveal the revived interest in the works of our great poets and artists and to remind their compatriots that Italy, in spite of all her political vicissitudes, was still the home of poetic inspiration. Coleridge, with his lectures on

Dante, Warton with his careful studies of our literature, and Gray, one of the most learned of English poets, with his letters and poems, revealed a true appreciation of Italy's classical beauties. Gray, frankly admitting that the opening lines of his *Elegy* are 'an echo of the divine Alighieri', was wont to say 'I by no means wish to have been born anything but an Englishman, yet I should rejoice to exchange tongues with Italy'.

The names of Byron, Shelley, Landor, Leigh Hunt, the Brownings, Ruskin and Swinburne are indissolubly connected with Italy. Their numerous visits and long sojourns in her various cities, their sympathy with her struggle for freedom and unity are so well known as hardly to require mention. Their works are full of reminiscences of this 'Magic Land' of Meredith which they loved with the hearts of artists and the imagination of poets. Many of their most famous works celebrate her monuments, her shrines, her landscapes, her heroes and her political aspirations. Those English singers had a profound admiration for our great thinkers, who influenced all their artistic creations from Byron's *Childe Harold* to the divine melodies of Shelley; from the impassioned verse of Keats to the *Amours de Voyage* of Clough; from the *Imaginary Conversations* of Landor to the ornate and eloquent prose of Ruskin and Pater, and from the revolutionary lines of Swinburne to the serene and philosophic poetry of Browning. Among the writers whose names are associated with Italy many lie buried beneath her sunny skies; Landor settled in Florence exclaiming, 'Italy is now my country'; Leigh Hunt found in Pisa a

AN OUTLINE OF CULTURAL RELATIONS

solace for his griefs; Shelley declared that the inspiration for his greatest poems came to him from the reawakening of spring in 'that divinest climate and the new life with which it drenches the spirits'; Keats basked in the sensuousness of the Italian atmosphere and, had he not died so young, would have become the most Italianate of English poets; Dante Gabriele Rossetti was from childhood fascinated by our primitives; Swinburne developed his ideals under the influence of Mazzini; and Ruskin, an ardent admirer of our arts, wrote many volumes in appreciation of her treasures and an eloquent commentary on the *Divina Commedia*.

Byron's residence in Italy was an event of the utmost importance in his life and in his work. He identified himself so completely with the spirit of the land of his adoption that he almost seems an Italian writing in English. He was the most passionate lover and most strenuous defender of our country; and, had a War of Italian Independence been possible at that time, he would undoubtedly have taken up arms as he did later for Greece. Byron must be considered as one of the poets of our *Risorgimento*. His invectives against Italy's 'barbaric foes' are the fiercest ever uttered by any poet; and his barbarians are not those of Imperial Rome but the foreign oppressors of Italy in modern times. Even among contemporary Italians it would have been difficult to find a tenderer expression of passionate love for 'fair Italy, the garden of the world, the home of all Art yields and Nature can decree'. We have ample evidence of his participation in the political movements of the time, his generous offers of financial assistance and the persecution he had to suffer. It is known that he espoused the cause of the Carbonari (in his cellars were stored their guns and ammunition) and for that reason he was obliged to depart from Ravenna and Rome. His friendship for the famous patriot and conspirator Pietro Gamba led him to take refuge with the Gambas in Pisa and share their exile from Tuscany. It was Pietro Gamba, too, who was the poet's inseparable companion in the Greek campaign.

Byron's letters prove how soon after his arrival in Italy he came under the spell of Pulci; and when he had successfully translated two books of the latter's *Morgante Maggiore* he repeatedly asserted his conviction that this was the best work he had ever done. Soon he adopted the metre and spirit of the Italian poet for an original work on a Venetian subject, calling it *Beppo: A Venetian Story*. Other English poets had already employed the *ottava rima*, had tried the same mingling of grave and gay which is characteristic of the style of Tuscany, but Byron's work had qualities of emotion and execution which were all his own. It is doubtful if he had himself previously realised his powers of comedy, but the fact remains that he never afterwards abandoned this style and it is to poems of this genre that he owes his most enduring fame.

The enthusiasm of Mrs. Browning for the political life and liberation of our country inspired the majority of her poems and, in particular, those verses entitled *From Casa Guidi Windows* into which she condenses her impressions of the revolutionary events which she witnessed in Tuscany. They form a simple and vivid account whose considerable value is due to the intensity with which those impressions were felt. For fifteen years of her married life she made her home in Florence, whose history and art were sources of the greatest interest and joy to her. In both her poems and letters she clearly shows the supreme place held in her heart by 'the most beautiful city ever built by man'. The innumerable allusions to the variety of its colours, to its churches, museums, squares, statues and to the traditions of the City of Flowers can only be fully understood and appreciated by those who have an intimate acquaintance with it.

The same may be said of Robert Browning himself. His poems like *Andrea del Sarto*, *Fra Lippo Lippi*, etc., are only obscure for those with an insufficient knowledge of the history of art. In these poems we find no obscurity of either thought or expression, and the same observation applies to the greater part of his poetic work. The most fascinating period of Browning's poetic life belongs without doubt to those years which he spent in the land of sunshine and beauty. Whoever would appreciate the highest achievements of the poet's thought and art must read the poems written during that period of life, joy and love in Italy. Her natural beauties, monuments and works of art were an inexhaustible fount of living inspiration for Browning who never wearied of proclaiming her his sole school and university. May students of the present generation re-echo the words of the old poet, 'My University is Italy, the land sacred to the muses and the gods'.

SHAKESPEARE AND ITALY

HIS SOURCES OF INSPIRATION AND MATERIAL

The laws of history teach us that great poets and artists are neither isolated phenomena nor the products of chance, but are preceded by a long preparatory period and are without exception the craftsmen who give the final touches to the great edifice, whose construction has been the work of centuries. When the material has been collected from all parts and when nothing remains but to classify it, then, at the psychological moment, appears the genius, whose ability to manipulate its various elements makes possible the creation of a sublime structure. His intervention is essential, because without him this material would soon lose its value and be condemned to oblivion. He alone gives to the elements at his disposal those qualities of surpassing merit which render them immortal. He alone, deriving his inspiration from his predecessors, at the same time perfects and adds lustre to their achievements.

In the course of the centuries, when all that prepares the way for the creative genius has vanished, artistic masterpieces may appear so sublime that we begin to doubt whether they can even be the work of mortal men. Modern criticism has sought to dispel this illusion by demonstrating the debt of greater or lesser magnitude which all masters owe to their predecessors, whether it be in the field of art, science or literature. Herculean efforts have been made to reconstruct the ages in which they lived; and, when it is found impossible to penetrate the mysteries of their times, recourse is had to conjecture. Thus have come to light the forerunners of Dante like those of Molière; Homer himself, though shrouded in the mists of centuries, has seen rise before him all the shades of his poetic and prophetic precursors, who even threaten his very existence as a real individual.

This research has also been made in the case of writers who lived nearer our own times and who will pass as our contemporaries when future generations admire them from the same distance as we to-day admire Homer, Virgil, Dante and the other fathers of modern culture.

Shakespeare himself has been subjected in modern times to criticism and dissection. Scholars have made a complete analysis of his sources and have employed the utmost diligence in their search for the works of which he made use. Hence we may now know the springs which fostered his genius, and we can point to the earlier writings from which he derived his inspiration, as well as to the countries where he sought his material. Some had asserted that Shakespeare was exceptionally ignorant, if not actually illiterate. Others declared him to be an inspired genius, owing little or nothing to the culture of the period or to the literatures of his own or preceding ages. Learned Englishmen rebelled at the very idea of Shakespearian erudition, reiterating indignantly that he who proclaimed the dramatist to have been also a scholar detracted from the glory of England.

HIS SOURCES OF INSPIRATION AND MATERIAL

This supposed contradiction between the education and the works of the poet has induced some to believe that the facts of Shakespeare's career are inconsistent with those of his literary successes. Thus a group of writers has arrived at the absurd conclusion that his dramas must have been written by men more learned than himself, and, in support of their theory, have put forward the name of Francis Bacon, without considering that this essayist could never claim to be either a poet or a dramatist. More recently other critics have asserted that most, if not all, of Shakespeare's plays were the work of Giovanni Florio, the translator of Montaigne and a teacher of Italian in London, the son of a Florentine reformer, who was a professor at Oxford during the latter part of the sixteenth century. But to anyone in the least familiar with the works of our English poet the opinions of these critics are without justification and utterly ridiculous.

Shakespeare was in reality the possessor of a vast store of learning; and in saying this we do justice not only to England but to the most illustrious of her sons. Besides his most fertile imaginative power he possessed the faculty of assimilating the characteristic details of the works which he read. Spenser, Milton, Byron, Browning and Tennyson all possessed the latter quality, but none of them to the same degree. In Shakespeare's case the assimilative faculty reinforced his imaginative fertility. He had made a profound study of the literature of his own time; and the fruits of his reading were immediately digested, assimilated, transformed by his powerful imagination; and when they reappeared in some concrete form they bore, with rare exceptions, the stamp of his individuality rather than the traces of their origin. The mind of Shakespeare might be compared to a sensitive photographic plate which had only to be turned towards any subject in life or literature for the merest fraction of a second in order to receive the impression of a picture which could be developed and reproduced at will.

Shakespeare's amazing familiarity with laws and legal formulae would induce us to believe that, at some period of his youth, he must have been apprenticed to a lawyer. Some consider that confirmation of this theory is to be found in lines published by the satirist, Thomas Nash, on those men of law who had abandoned their profession for love of poetry. Shakespeare delights in displaying his knowledge of legal expressions; he knows the jargon of the courts and the technical terms of jurisprudence. While many English writers of the period are frequently incorrect in their references to the laws of matrimony, inheritance and commerce, modern jurists in the course of all their investigations have never succeeded in finding an error of this kind in Shakespeare.

The poet is equally familiar with the theories concerning every aspect of human life. If from his knowledge of law we may conclude that he practised as a lawyer, then from his typographical allusions we may infer that he also worked as a printer. In *Shakespeare and the Art of Printing*, we are told that if the poet had spent his whole life in a printer's establishment he could not have learned with greater precision the many peculiarities of nomenclature belonging to that trade. And the Bishop of Salisbury, nephew of William Wordsworth, in his work—*Shakespeare and the Bible*—declares that the poet is richly endowed with the biblical spirit, and that he himself has often been profoundly surprised by the marvellous facility with which the dramatist employs biblical forms and expressions, sometimes reproducing with rare felicity the style and spirit of the Holy Scriptures.

Of the natural sciences Shakespeare had a thorough knowledge. Studies have been published to prove his familiarity with the life of insects; and Morgan, in his *Shakespearian Myth* asserted that the poet's knowledge of the characteristics of mammiferous animals was inexhaustible. It is easy to demonstrate also that he was versed in the study of plants. Greater still is the wonder aroused by his opinions in other provinces of science—in physics and chemistry, for example. In a volume entirely devoted to the poet's familiarity with the study of medicine, the author, Professor Bucknell, attributes to him an acquaintance with the discoveries of many of the most illustrious scientists of our times. His representation of madness surpasses the descriptions of all other poets. Alienists are filled with admiration for the accurate descriptions of the symptoms of insanity in Lear and Ophelia. It seems that Shakespeare anticipated the more intelligent modern methods of caring for the insane—methods radically opposed to the barbarous treatments prevalent in his own time. Nor was he ignorant of the subject of Medical Jurisprudence; indeed his acquaintance with all the sciences far surpassed that of any of his contemporaries. In some parts of the plays we find frequent allusions to the circulation of the blood, although Harvey's work was not published until 1628. We must admit, however, that Harvey's master, Cisalpino di Padua, had propounded his theory of circulation as early as 1590.

We know that the laws of gravity were discovered by Newton, who was born in 1642, and that the general idea of gravitation towards the centre of the earth was unknown before Kepler, who discovered the third law of the motion of heavenly bodies, two years after the death of Shakespeare. Yet the poet distinctly refers to the theory in *Troilus and Cressida*:

> Time, force, and death,
> Do to this body what extremes you can;
> But the strong base and building of my love
> Is as the very centre of the earth,
> Drawing all things to it.

Shakespeare also had some notion of geology, though the foundations of this science were only laid by Niels Steno, born in 1638. After a study of all these facts we are inclined to believe that anyone who doubts Shakespeare's learning and culture must himself possess but little of either.

The poet's works reveal his lively interest in the narratives and characters of classical poetry and his delight in the traditions of both mythical and historical times. We are often surprised at the way in which he introduces all the conventional themes of classical poetry, as well as the principal episodes of Greek

HIS SOURCES OF INSPIRATION AND MATERIAL

history. Besides the scenes of his dramas which are laid in Athens, the names of many Greek heroes from Agamemnon, Ulysses, Nestor and Theseus to Alcibiades and Pericles demonstrate his love for the history and his interest in the evolution of Hellenic civilisation. Whether or not Greek was taught in the schools of Stratford, we certainly find in the plays of Shakespeare many phrases reminiscent of the Greek tragedies. Some of these coincidences are profoundly striking. In the *Electra* of Sophocles the Chorus consoles Electra for the supposed death of Orestes with the same expressions of sympathy as those addressed to Hamlet on the death of his father by his mother and uncle. A parallel to the passage where Antisthenes declares that he sleeps more soundly amidst the discomforts of poverty than the rich Athenians do in their luxury is to be found in *Henry IV*, Part II, Act III, scene i, where the King speaks of the thousands who find repose easy while he tosses sleepless in his palace. The precise coincidence of these and many other passages leads us to believe that they are not accidental but due to a reading of Greek works, and that the language itself was not unknown to the poet. His acquaintance with the Latin language and literature cannot be doubted. A large part of his mythology is derived from Ovid's *Metamorphoses*; and not only is he acquainted with the most important episodes of the poem but he knows every part of the fifteen books. That the dramatic qualities of the Latin poet appealed to Shakespeare is evident from the latter's frequent allusions to Arianna, Leda and Hecuba, for instance, and also his quotations from the first Epistle of the same author which we find in *The Taming of the Shrew.*

The two poems—*Venus and Adonis* and *The Rape of Lucrece*—for which the author derived his inspiration from the sweet and tender sentiments of the Italian Renaissance, are of prime importance to us. From Ovid is taken the Latin motto prefixed to the former poem, which is in fact merely an amplification of a scene in the *Metamorphoses*; whilst the *Ars Amandi* explains the poet's acquaintance with many details of a private character, for example, the intrigue of Mars and Venus, which inspired Juliet's frank assertion:

> At lovers' perjuries,
> They say, Jove laughs.

In his *Rape of Lucrece* the poet followed the general lines of the graceful version of Lucretia's story in the *Fasti*, and from the second book of Virgil's *Aeneid* he took the description of the Sack of Troy, the stratagem of Sinon, the death of Priam and the grief of the abandoned Dido—extraordinary and sensational episodes which reveal the poet's taste in the early years of his literary career. There are many other passages, especially in *Hamlet*, which lead us to believe that the *Aeneid* exercised for some time a considerable fascination over him.

In *The Comedy of Errors* Shakespeare faithfully reproduces the humour and vivacity of Plautus, and on many occasions puts Latin phrases and expressions into the mouths of his characters, as is the case in *The Taming of the Shrew*, in *Love's Labour's Lost* and in *The Merry Wives of Windsor.* Besides the writers already mentioned there are indications in Shakespeare's plays that he must have read Terence, Horace, Juvenal, Seneca and Plutarch; and not only does he know the works of the classical Roman authors but he also manifests a certain familiarity with the great Latin writers of the Italian Renaissance; for example, Sannazzaro, Vida and Fracastoro, to some of whom he refers with special sympathy, as in the case of the poet Battista Mantuano, to whom he affectionately alludes in the phrase: 'good old Mantuan' (*Love's Labour's Lost*, Act IV, scene ii).

There are those who hold that Shakespeare was simply an unlearned actor, and who argue that he was ignorant of the rules of prosody, because he sometimes erred in the quantities of syllables, or accented those which are normally unaccented. This supposed ignorance on the dramatist's part is in reality derived from a profound study of poetic art, together with a thorough knowledge of literary 'tricks of the trade'. These so-called errors are merely instances of poetic licence, such as are frequently found not only in Shakespeare but in those writers who are most versed in the works of the ancient Greeks and Romans. We find them indeed in Dante, Petrarch, Leopardi and, in more recent times, in Carducci and D'Annunzio.

Even the most casual readers of Shakespeare cannot fail to note the fact that the names of many of his characters are Italian, and that scenes in his dramas are often laid in one of the cities of Italy. Knowing little of the conditions prevailing in that period and nothing at all of Italian literature, they are astonished and seek an explanation. If, their curiosity being awakened, they carry their researches further, they will find that the chief dramatist of the English Renaissance, instead of inventing the stories which have entertained Europe for three centuries, was indebted not only for names, characters and scenes but also for entire plots and general inspiration to Italian books imported from Venice, Rome and Florence.

Amazed at this discovery the student begins to waver in his opinion of Shakespeare, and wonders how much would remain if all extraneous borrowed elements were eliminated from the plays. In that case, he thinks, we should have neither *Othello* nor *Romeo and Juliet*; we should lose by far the greater part of *The Merchant of Venice, Much Ado About Nothing, Twelfth Night, Measure for Measure* and *Cymbeline*; all life and interest would vanish from *The Tempest, The Taming of the Shrew* and *The Merry Wives of Windsor*; and we should have to renounce any claim to *The Two Gentlemen of Verona, All's Well That Ends Well* and *The Comedy of Errors*. He finds that all these dramas are wholly or partly derived from Italian works, and goes on to speculate where Shakespeare could have turned for his material if these works had not existed. Would he have been obliged to have recourse to arid national chronicles, to rough rustic ballads or to tales collected in the taverns and ale-houses of London? It is unnecessary to apologise for the procedure of our dramatist, because he acted in the wisest possible way; and if he had not adopted this course deliberately he would certainly have done it involuntarily.

HIS SOURCES OF INSPIRATION AND MATERIAL

Like all his English contemporaries Shakespeare was fascinated by Italy. Here he found the best material for his tragedies and romantic comedies. The discovery of his indebtedness to Italian sources need in no way diminish our good opinion of him. All poets copy, all imitate, all are to some extent plagiarists. Their greatness does not consist in creation or invention, but in giving life and movement to inert material. Like the other English poet who last century made this touching declaration of love for our country:

> Italy, my Italy!
>   Open my heart and you will see
>   Graved inside of it, 'Italy'.

Shakespeare evinces a varied and profound knowledge of the country in general and of our cities in particular. His writings display the breadth of his sympathy for Italy throughout the whole course of her glorious career. The loveliest lyrical passages in his plays are of purest Italian inspiration. There is no poet, with the exception of Dante, who has loved our land more ardently than the great English dramatist. Innumerable are the passages where he speaks of the special characteristics of our peninsula, of her history and of her customs. He knew that Padua possessed a great university and was the majestic Alma Mater of the arts.

>   for the great desire I had
> To see fair Padua, nursery of arts,
> I am arrived for fruitful Lombardy,
> The pleasant garden of great Italy . . .

He knew that Padua with all its learning was under the protection of Venice and that Mantua was not. Besides he assigns special and precise attributes to various cities, e.g. Pisa, renowned for her wealth but still more for her 'grave citizens', an expression used by Dante; Milan is 'the fair' and possesses a 'royal court' and the famous St. Gregory Well. Elsewhere he speaks of the Florentines and Neapolitans, and accuses the inhabitants of Pisa of being avaricious. He knew that the Florentines were notable merchants and mathematicians, making frequent use in their commerce of letters of credit and counting their money by ducats; and he was also aware that they were constantly in conflict with the Sienese. And here the poet uses a phrase which is pure Italian—The Florentines and the Sienese are by the ear (*si pigliano per gli orecchi*). Apart from all the references to Italy in general which are about 800, and to Rome which are about 400, we find that the most important Italian cities are mentioned in the following order of frequency—Venice 52 times, Naples 34, Milan 25, Florence 23, Padua 22 and Verona 20. Then follow Genoa, Mantua, Pisa, Ferrara and others.

SHAKESPEARE AND HIS ITALIAN CRITICS

It has been asserted that Voltaire was the first to call the attention of Europe to the works of Shakespeare; but long before the appearance of his *Lettres Philosophiques* the Italians had shown an interest in the great English dramatist. Gregorio Leti in 1683, speaking of Shakespeare, said that 'the splendid and magnificent English theatres deserved to be seen by foreigners, because in all that concerned scenes of comedy, the skill of the actors, invention and design, and in every other respect, they were in advance of all the theatres of Europe'. Megalotti, who in 1692 visited England and translated John Philips' *Cyder*, also wrote a few pages on the English dramatist; and in 1705 Apostolo Zeno composed a musical drama entitled *Amleto*, based on the English play, which was translated into English and given at the Haymarket Theatre in 1712. Maffei, the celebrated author of *Merope*, who visited England in 1713, declared that Shakespeare was 'one of the sources of the finest English poetry'.

About the same time two other Italians were attracted by the Shakespearian plays: the scientist, Antonio Conti, one of the most learned men of his time, and the poet, Paolo Rolli, a teacher of Italian language and literature at the English Court. They had become acquainted with the plays of the poet at the time when the Duke of Buckingham, following the bad taste of some contemporary critics, tried to modernise *Julius Caesar* in accordance with the canons of the *Illuminati*. This attempt fascinated Conti, who was induced by it to study the works of Shakespeare and thus came to conceive a new admiration for Tragedy. His judgment of the English poet is remarkable if we consider the period in which he lived. 'Shakespeare,' he wrote, 'is the Corneille of England, but much more irregular than Corneille, though equally full of great ideas and noble sentiments. I shall only mention his *Julius Caesar*. The poet makes him die in the Third Act; the rest of the tragedy is taken up with Mark Antony's speech, and with the war and deaths of Cassius and Brutus. Could there be a greater violation of the Unities? But the English before *Cato* treated Aristotle's rules with contempt, for the aim of Tragedy was to please and the best dramatist was he who was most successful in this.'

The poet Rolli in his *Life of Milton* remarked that Shakespeare by his tragedies raised English drama to a matchless sublimity. Rolli appears to have been familiar with the latter's works, for in his *Essay on the Epic Poetry Of European Nations* he refers to *Henry IV* and *Richard III* and declares that 'what will make Shakespeare shine forever upon the English stage is the strength of painting in the characters of the great English and Roman heroes he sets forth in his historical tragedies, so skilfully represented in their virtues, tempers and faults that they seem to live'. He adds that Voltaire had never read or seen *The Tempest* or *Macbeth*, which, according to the Italian critic, is the best of the tragedies. The whole of this judgment may be summed up in two words: 'beauty' and 'irregularity'. Here we have the substance of almost all the verdicts on the poet reiterated monotonously both in France and Italy. There is, therefore, no need to resort to Voltaire, as is usually done, to discover the reason for so much uniformity in the European criticism of Shakespearian drama in the eighteenth century.

In 1735 we note a touch of acerbity in Algarotti's criticism: 'Innumerable faults and inimitable thoughts.' Quadrio was even more severe: 'Instead of bringing credit to the English theatre by correcting its defects, Shakespeare led it to utter ruin. And though in the monstrous farces that go by the name of tragedies we find some brilliant and beautiful scenes, together with some great and awe-inspiring characteristics, yet even these are probably outside the bounds of literary rules and lacking in orderliness and good taste.' These critics were followed by Baretti, who had already written on many problems connected with the theatre. In order to know Shakespeare better and to be able to speak of him more authoritatively he went to England, where a renewed enthusiasm for the study of the English theatre was encouraged by Dr. Johnson, one of Baretti's intimate friends. The English literary environment in which the Italian writer found himself indubitably encouraged and developed his admiration for Shakespeare. Baretti mentions the dramatist for the first time in his dissertation upon Italian poetry, written in answer to the arguments of Voltaire, who had spoken with contempt of the great poets of Italy. In this work he asserts that the Italian poets had received the admiration of both the learned and the ignorant, a tribute that only Homer, Shakespeare, Corneille and very few others had been paid. In the Preface to his *Dictionary*, Baretti eulogised the English language and literature; and, in order to encourage their study in Italy, he made a digression on the great English poet. He praised the power of language and the fertility of imagination in Shakespeare, Spenser, Dryden and other immortals, who, combining the purity and freshness of Greek poetry, the beauty of Latin, the charm of Italian and the brilliancy of French with the vigour and extravagance of the German, had inaugurated a new fashion of poetic thinking. He concluded that it was impossible for him to translate these authors, not so much on account of his own inexperience, as of the difference in the spirit of the two languages, which prevented him from giving to his fellow-countrymen the best products of the northern genius.

Wishing to provide Italian literature with a fresh stimulus he offered in his critical review, *La Frusta*, models of vigorous English literature as a contrast to the over-effeminate works produced in France. Here again he entered into controversy with French writers in general, and with Voltaire in particular, who was the main target of his criticism. It cannot be said that in *La Frusta* Baretti extolled the glory of Shakespeare; but, whenever the occasion presented itself, he put him forward as a model worthy of study, and endeavoured to mitigate the hostility of his Latin contemporaries. He began by attacking the popular opinion that Shakespeare was a confused mass of beauties and defects;

and seized this opportunity to demonstrate how great was the ignorance of English literature on the part of Voltaire, who from his literary throne dared to dictate to Europe. 'Shakespeare,' said Baretti, 'both in Tragedy and Comedy, is a poet who stands alone against all the Corneilles, the Racines and the Molières of France, whose work cannot be compared with *Othello*, *King Lear* or *Hamlet*.' He went on to record the boundless praise given to the dramas of the English poet, and concluded by saying that he fully agreed with the French critics that there are many faults in Shakespeare, but that he could detect also an amazing number of beauties; and that a single one of Shakespeare's beauties surpassed anything to be found in French literature. In other respects he did not despise the French dramatists; he would have given one finger to have been able to write *Cinna*, but two to be able to create a character like Caliban in *The Tempest*.

Here Baretti approached the point of view of German Romantic Criticism in the nineteenth century. Latin critics for the most part admired the historical tragedies, and in the other four great tragedies they commonly admired only the pompous and solemn characters that bore some resemblance to the grandiose models of classical tragedy. Baretti, on the contrary, fixed his attention on three characters little noted at that time— Caliban, Shylock and Falstaff—as creations of the awe-inspiring genius of the north. This attitude became so common among the romantic critics that they were later reproached for admiring only the deformed and the abnormal; but in the middle of the eighteenth century these opinions were a daring novelty in France and in Italy. Baretti with equal skill ridiculed the adherents of the three unities, in order to show from yet another point of view the greatness of the English dramatist. In this particular field he was far bolder than Metastasio, Johnson or Lessing who showed some hesitation, either practical or theoretical, in their condemnation of this convention. Despite Baretti's spirited defence, Italian literary taste in the eighteenth century, as Carducci rightly observed, expressed itself on the whole in adoration of Pope and indifference to Shakespeare. In 1756 Valentini published the first translation of *Julius Caesar* and in 1769 Pignotti wrote a short poem on *The Tomb of the English Poet*, in which occur lines describing Shakespeare's 'unhappy art which dares to challenge Nature herself in the mighty effort to imprison and enslave her'. About the same time Paradisi wrote that in the English dramatist he found beauties, 'but also too many and too great faults'. And De Gamerra, who in his domestic tragedy, *The Guilty Mother*, boasts of having combined the boldness of Shakespeare with the ingenious intrigue of Lope de Vega, wrote that 'the English dramatist produced a type of tragedy free from the trammels of rules and embellished with a sublime, pathetic, picturesque and vivacious imagination. He evokes admiration, but a short-lived admiration, for portraits exhibiting all the greatness and nobility of Raphael are followed by miserable examples unworthy of a great artist.'

We cannot pass over the opinions of two other famous men of letters, Bettinelli and Cesarotti, both admirers of Voltaire. They translated into Italian some of his dramatic works and wrote various essays on the theatre. Bettinelli, when publishing his own tragedies in 1771, prefaced them with a Dissertation on the Italian Theatre, and in another edition added as an Appendix four Dialogues on the Modern Theatre. In the first of these Dialogues he complains that Melpomene, following the bad taste of the northern peoples, delights in scenes of horror. He pours scorn on Monti, who in his *Aristodemo* had made use of some scenes and ideas from Shakespeare's *Richard III*, and declares himself disgusted by the dreadful characterisation of the English dramatist. Cesarotti expressed similar ideas. After translating the *Caesar* of Voltaire he prefixed to it an essay in which he thus reasons: 'The English tragedy of Shakespeare under this title might have been more reasonably called *The Roman Republic*, because it is nothing but the history of a Roman revolution. This drama does not recommend itself by its form or by the development of its plot and it is not to be compared with the others. It derives its worth mainly from the enthusiasm of the poet and from the vigour of the style.'

It is evident that Cesarotti still possessed enough magnanimity to attribute to poor Shakespeare some merit of a minor kind; but hardly is the merit admitted than faults are discovered. Indeed he soon adds that even vigour of style disappears at intervals, degenerating more than once into baseness; and he concludes with the statement that the productions of this great and polished genius are, like the Colossus of Nabucco, composed of a mixture of the most precious jewels and of the basest metal. He recognises that the most notable part of Shakespeare's *Julius Caesar* is the speech of Antony over Caesar's body and compares it with the corresponding passage in Voltaire in order to demonstrate once more the superiority of the French poet. Not content with expressing his ideas on this subject in Italian, Cesarotti felt impelled to render them into Latin in a composition on tragic poets entitled *Mercurius*. It must be remembered that Bettinelli had also attacked the sacred fame of Dante; that Bettinelli and Cesarotti were friends and admirers of Voltaire; and that, if they did not actually owe to him their knowledge of the English dramatist, it can be safely affirmed that in Italy literary likes and dislikes were at that time influenced by the libels of the French poet.

This type of criticism was greatly modified with the growth of English influence in Italy towards the end of the eighteenth century and the beginning of the nineteenth, and with the rise of romantic writers like Manzoni, Pellico and Niccolini, whose attitude towards the dramatist was inspired by love and enthusiasm. But old prejudices still lingered; and during the first half of the nineteenth century we can trace in Italy three trends of opinion regarding Shakespeare: the first unreservedly enthusiastic, the second holding Shakespearian drama to be a 'mixture of beauties and defects' whilst the third was uncompromisingly antagonistic. 'A great revolution is taking place in the literature and the taste of the people,' wrote Niccolini in 1835. 'The days of Racine's classical tragedies are over, nor does

Shakespeare's romantic tragedy seem to suit the age. A great man is wanted to solve the problem and I do not believe that I am he. The author must educate the public, and the public the actors. Where is the public and where are the actors in Italy?'

SHAKESPEARE ON THE ITALIAN STAGE

Italian actors contributed greatly to familiarise Italy and Europe with the name and works of Shakespeare, having excelled the artists of every other continental country in the interpretation of the poet on the stage. In France, Spain and Germany there has never been a Lady Macbeth or a Juliet like Adelaide Ristori; a Desdemona like Clementina Cazzola; an Othello or Macbeth like Ermete Zacconi; a Petruchio or Shylock like Ermete Novelli; nor has there ever been an Ernesto Rossi or a Tommaso Salvini, the first and greatest of the Shakespearian interpreters in Italy, unequalled in the characters of Romeo, Hamlet, Lear and Othello.

Before Rossi and Salvini few actors had been successful in their attempts to stage Shakespeare's dramas in Italy. A tragedy entitled *Hamlet*, founded upon Shakespeare's, was given for nine nights at the theatre of S. Crisostomo in Venice during the Carnival of 1774, and in the summer of the following year was repeated in several Italian cities. Monti tells us that in 1779 he shed tears in a public theatre over a *Romeo and Juliet* and went home horror-stricken after Hamlet's outburst of passion; and Mrs. Piozzi (the former Mrs. Thrale) wrote that in 1785 she was unlucky enough to miss at Padua a performance of *Romeo and Juliet*, which was acted there amidst great applause under the title of *Tragedia Veronese*. In 1790 a *Hamlet* by Caruso was played in Florence; and at the close of the century Marrochesi, while still a young man, produced a *Hamlet* in the little theatre of Borgognissanti; at the same time Lombardi was producing *Othello* at Venice while Da Ponte in Vienna took material for his libretti from Shakespeare's comedies.

Nor was Shakespeare neglected by the Italian ballet writers. In 1773 S. Severino produced in Berlin an opera based on *Romeo and Juliet* and others soon followed. Salieri composed an opera entitled *Falstaff* in Vienna in 1798. The poet's name was made familiar to the Italian provincial towns by a number of ballets derived from his works. In Sicily *I Due Spettri Al Convito* by Francesco Clerico long enjoyed great popularity. The piece is a tragic ballet in five acts in which at the banquet the ghosts of Duncan and Banquo accuse Macbeth of their respective murders. Antonio Cherubini in 1830 produced in Milan *Le Tombe di Verona* based on *Romeo and Juliet*, and Salvatore Vigano, a prolific composer of ballets, modelled his tragic dances mainly on the works of the English dramatist; two of them, *Coriolanus* and *Othello*, were greatly admired. But these ballets, which preceded Verdi's *Falstaff*, *Othello* and *Macbeth* as well as the operas of Rossini and Leoncavallo, were merely adaptations of Shakespeare's works, and offended the good taste of the poet's admirers, so that Monti wrote indignantly of a wretched mangling of Shakespeare's great tragedy of *Hamlet* presented to the Milanese in 1817. Nevertheless they continued until Gustavo Modena and his pupils began to give regular performances of the English dramatist on the Italian stage.

Gustavo Modena was a very distinguished actor, a man with artistic ideals and the necessary taste for reforming the stage. He is considered the father of the modern school of actors in Italy, of which Rossini, Salvini, Ermete Novelli and Zacconi were the most illustrious representatives. After producing some plays of Schiller with success at Venice in 1843, he attempted *Othello* in the Teatro del Re in Milan, at that time one of the best theatres in Italy. Anxious to give something new he adapted a translation of *Othello*, which he thought suitable for presentation to the people, taking endless pains with the staging. The result was disastrous. In the scene between Iago and Roderigo, when the latter begins to shout in the street outside Brabantio's house, the audience began to whisper. They had gone to the theatre to hear a tragedy and they seemed to be listening to a scene from one of Goldoni's comedies or even to a farce. A regular uproar followed and the curtain had to be lowered amid a storm of hissing.

In the first half of the nineteenth century, despite the efforts of his translators, Shakespeare was still little read in Italy. The translations of his works were confined to a very narrow circle and were practically unknown to the general public. To men of letters Shakespeare seemed harsh and extravagant. Many repeated the daring criticism of Voltaire, who, in order to convey the impression that he himself was the only man of genius, despised Dante as a writer lacking poetic power and called Shakespeare 'wild and drunken'. Opinions differed: sometimes perplexed, sometimes adverse.

Stylists discussed Shakespeare in the spirit in which Bembo, Della Casa and the rhetoricians of the Renaissance discussed Dante, pouring scorn on the Florentine poet, because he seemed to them a barbarian who had made use of coarse and improper language. In the books of precepts intended to develop the literary taste of young students harsh criticism was passed on the English poet and certain splendid passages of his tragedies were quoted as examples of a style fantastic, vulgar and grotesquely extravagant. It is the old story of human error—man despising what transcends his comprehension; it needs a new generation to understand a new form of beauty and to reveal its full meaning.

But soon after Gustavo Modena had produced *Othello* and *Hamlet* on the stage, public opinion began to change in Italy. Piccinini relates that one afternoon he was strolling along the streets of Florence with the famous philologist, Pietro Fanfani, whose reputation had already spread all over the peninsula. Suddenly this man of letters said to him: 'Do you know, I have been reading Shakespeare's *Othello* lately? It has many beauties. I admire it. I am convinced that Shakespeare was no fool as a writer.' This makes evident the attitude of the average man of letters towards the poet, and it is also sufficient to convince us of the extent to which stage actors can be true educators, since the greatest of Italian actors were most enthusiastic in popularising throughout Europe the literature and the culture of Shakespeare.

Ernesto Rossi was the first to interpret Shakespeare successfully upon the Italian stage. He learned English and paid a visit to London to see Charles Kean in *Richard II*. He was well received by the English actor, who gave him acting versions of *Hamlet*, *Othello* and other plays. In the spring of 1856 he fulfilled his great ambition by playing *Othello* in Milan. The performance met with some success and was repeated several times. A fortnight later he produced *Hamlet* with equal success. In 1858 Rossi played Macbeth at Venice and Lear at Turin. Lear was one of his best parts and won him admiration even in London. Coriolanus, Shylock and Romeo were among his other successful rôles. Rossi has left us proofs of his love for the English dramatist in the prose translation of *Julius Caesar*, in his *Studî Drammatici*, in the studies of Shakespearian characters and in the work he published under the title of *Quarant'Anni di Vita Artistica*. He even called his villa 'Shakespeare'.

Salvini was a far greater actor. At first he felt no attraction towards Shakespeare. Then a work of the dramatist fell into his hands, and its forms, characters and thought struck him as so strange that he hesitated whether he should study him or not. Encouraged however by Rossi's success, and after a long period of study and preparation, he decided to produce *Othello* for the first time at Vicenza, choosing that tragedy for a performance for his own benefit. Clementina Cazzola and Piccinini, the latter unsurpassed in Italy as Iago, played with him in this first performance. The quality of the company was excellent; every care had been taken with the costumes, which were faultless; suitable scenery had been prepared by a scene-painter of ability and the production of the play was awaited with lively interest. Salvini being already a very popular artist, a great public assembled in his honour and greeted him with prolonged applause. But as it was the first time that a tragedy of that kind had been seen in Vicenza, popular judgment wavered as to the artistic merit of the work. From Vicenza Salvini went to Venice where his rendering of Othello met with the same reception. There was applause, there were calls before the curtain; but the general public was not satisfied and as they left the house voiced their disapproval saying: 'No, such things are not for us.' This did not discourage the actor who, little by little, first in one city then in another, with his wonderful power did more to educate the taste of the public than many professional teachers, and much more than certain men of letters had hitherto done.

'It will be easily believed,' wrote Salvini himself, 'that I made little account of this mistaken judgment or criticism, and repeated the play several times, until at last they found some good in it. At Rome I forced the play on public favour. A sure sign that it commanded interest was that there was a full house. It was not to their taste it is true—but they could not stay away. For four seasons I always selected that play for my benefit. The first time people blamed me; the second they began to be interested; the third they were pleased, and after that every time I went to Rome they asked me how soon I should give *Othello*.'

We may affirm that Salvini's supreme acting threw into relief every beauty and even discovered beauties hitherto unknown in the Shakespearian masterpieces. A true interpretation such as his was like a dazzling flash of light, so unexpectedly were the greatest depths of the soul revealed. 'I heard Salvini and Clementina Cazzola for the first time', said a critic, 'in *Othello* at the Niccolini Theatre in Florence. And I recall the deep impression they made on me. I did not feel that I was attending a play; my youthful imagination, strengthened by the supreme ability of the actors, made me feel that all that had taken place on the stage was real; and when at the end I saw Othello and Desdemona reappear to thank the public, holding each other's hands, it seemed to me impossible that these two should now smile at each other and be thus united and at peace.'

Salvini tried every possible means of reproducing Othello's racial characteristics. 'At Gibraltar I spent my time', he wrote, 'studying the Moors. I was much struck by one very fine figure, majestic in gait and romantic in face except for a slight projection of the lower lip. The man's colour was between copper and coffee, not very dark, and he had a slight moustache and scanty curled hair on his chin. Up to that time I had always made up Othello simply with a moustache, but after seeing that superb Moor I added the hair on the chin, and sought to copy his gestures, movements and carriage. Had I been able I should have imitated his voice too, so closely did that splendid Moor represent to me the true type of the Shakespearian hero. Othello must have been a son of Mauretania, for what else could the author have intended to imply but that the Moor was returning to his native land?'

One evening in 1865 the dramatic critic, Celestino Bianchi, much respected for his learning and genius, was present at a performance of *Hamlet* given by Salvini. On leaving the theatre this writer, who had lived all his life among artists, exclaimed: 'This evening I understood things in *Hamlet* which hitherto had escaped me.' Lord Normanby, the British ambassador to the Court of Italy, a man specially interested in dramatic art, having formerly acted in his castle in England with Edmund Kean, declared that Salvini's *Hamlet* was the only one that would be generally accepted in all parts of the world; and Browning wrote to Salvini: 'During your play on Friday the entire lyre of tragedy resounded magnificently.' Nor did their verdict prove to be mistaken, for Salvini's *Hamlet* was acclaimed as both powerful and original in France, Germany and England.

When Salvini with his actors reached London for the first time he was seized by a kind of terror. Would he be able to touch and inspire those millions of hearts? He had hardly arrived when he noticed the bills on the hoardings of the city announcing the seventy-second night of *Hamlet* at the Lyceum Theatre, with Sir Henry Irving in the title rôle. Salvini was anxious to see and hear the illustrious English artist in that part, and after some hesitation he secured a box and went to the Lyceum. He was recognised by nobody; and, remaining as it were concealed in his box, he had a good opportunity of satisfying his curiosity. He arrived at the theatre a little late, so that he missed the scene of Hamlet in presence of the Ghost of his Father, the scene which in his judgment contained the best clue to the understanding of that strange character, and from which all the synthetic ideas of Hamlet are developed, but was in time to hear the last words of the oath of secrecy.

The Italian actor was struck by the excellence of the stage setting. There was a perfect imitation of the effect of moonlight, which at certain times flooded the stage with its rays or left it in darkness. Every detail was faultlessly and exactly reproduced. The curtain was again raised and Hamlet began his allusions, his rallies of sarcasm, his sententious sayings, his points of satire with the courtiers, who sought to study and to penetrate the sentiments of the young prince. 'In this scene Irving was sublime; his mobile face mirrored his thoughts, the subtle penetration of his phrases, so perfect in shading and incisiveness, showed him to be a master of his art. I do not believe', wrote Salvini, 'there is an actor who can stand beside him in this respect and I was so much impressed by it, so much intimidated by the art and powers of the consummate artist that at the end of the second act I said to myself: "I will not play Hamlet, my manager can say what he likes, but I will not play it," and I said it with the fullest resolution, so perfectly was the nature and the personality of the hero characterised, and with as much subtlety as there is philosophy in the part.

SHAKESPEARE ON THE ITALIAN STAGE

'Irving's acting of Hamlet was superb, but it never completely satisfied even the most generous of English critics. He gave an excellent interpretation of Hamlet's thoughts and reproduced those aspects of Hamlet's character which he found in himself, yet he did not perhaps render adequately the comic and sarcastic qualities of the play, which are to be counted among its beauties. But his Hamlet was exceedingly popular and crowds invariably gathered in front of the Lyceum hours before the play began. In the monologue, "To be, or not to be", Irving was admirable; in the scene with Ophelia he was deserving of the highest praise, in that with the players he was moving and in all this part of the play he appeared to my eyes to be the most perfect interpreter of that eccentric character. But further it was not so, and for the sake of art I regretted it.

'From the time when the passion assumes a deeper hue, and reasoning moderates impulses which are forcibly curbed, Irving seemed to me to show mannerism and to be strained and lacking in power; and it is not in him alone that I find this fault, but in nearly all foreign actors. There seems to be a limit of passion within which they remain true in their rendering of nature. But beyond that limit they become transformed and take on conventionality in their intonations, exaggeration in gestures and mannerism in their bearing. I then left my box saying to myself: "I can do Hamlet and I will try it".'

Salvini acted for the first time at Drury Lane in *Othello*. He did not wish to hasten his arrangements for the playing of Hamlet, lest he should appear to be challenging his rival, Sir Henry Irving, who was drawing crowds to the Lyceum. His *Othello* ran for thirty-two evenings. There were present many who had heard Edmund Kean's Othello and among them several professional critics. In the crowded theatre the *élite* of London society was always to be found. The Italian actor was discussed in every club and at every gathering. Adelina Patti, who was singing at Covent Garden, found public attention distracted and became jealous of his success. Sarah Bernhardt, whom the Italian actor had often criticised and in whom signs of envy and resentment could be detected, declared that he was the master of all modern actors.

Later Salvini played Hamlet for about a fortnight. Hundreds of columns were written on his interpretations of this tragedy. English critics discuss every new Shakespearian actor with exceptional minuteness. But Shakespeare in Britain is what Dante is in Italy. Pedantry plants roots round the works of these men of genius and would suffocate them, but in vain, for new life constantly springs from them overwhelming the surrounding parasites. Salvini did not escape criticism, but it was admitted that he had perceived and even revealed certain Shakespearian beauties hitherto unknown. Irving himself was advised to go to him for theory and instruction. Clement Scott, the theatrical critic, thought Salvini's interpretations of Hamlet's death the most beautiful he had ever seen, and Lewes proclaimed him the greatest actor in the world. In his Hamlet as in his Othello, Coriolanus, King Lear, and other performances were found flashes of genius, poetic power, rare versatility, accompanied by a wonderful unity and continuity of style. His interpretations were new and impressively original. In him was observed a very rare balance between genius for acting and those natural gifts which contributed greatly to the success of his interpretations. Great actors like Charles Kean, Wilson Barrett, Forbes-Robertson and Beerbohm Tree imitated not a few of Salvini's qualities. Even Sir Henry Irving made use of some of the Italian actor's innovations, especially in the death scene where Salvini was by the most severe critics judged to be unique and unsurpassable.

Salvini's acting stirred an enthusiasm never witnessed since the time of Rachel and Edmund Kean. English actors were so impressed that they came to regard him as their master. They sent him a petition signed by all the most distinguished members of the profession beseeching the privilege of hearing him at least in *Othello*. We can read the signatures of 451 actors belonging to twenty-five theatres. Salvini complied with the wishes of his colleagues. On the appointed day all the actors and actresses found themselves gathered together for the first time in their lives. The success of the performance was immense; Salvini could only say that he never played Othello so well as on this occasion. 'It seemed that all my talents were redoubled and sharpened. How I should have liked to act always as I did then.' Salvini became the most popular dramatic artist in Europe and America. He and his actors may claim to have deserved well of Shakespearian studies in Italy, Spain, France and Russia, where *Othello*, *Hamlet*,

Macbeth, *King Lear* and *Coriolanus* did not excite the same admiration as in England.

When in 1877 Salvini announced in Paris the performance of *Macbeth*, *Othello* and *Hamlet* there was a revival of curiosity and expectancy. Shakespeare seldom appealed to the Parisian public. Even some notable men of letters ignored or condemned him, some without having read his poetry or his prose. Victor Hugo and his friends, including Théophile Gautier and Paul de Saint Victor, had written some admirable pages on the English dramatist; Victor Hugo had explained much that appeared obscure in the immortal plays; his son had given a beautiful translation of the English dramatist; and Paul de Saint Victor had glorified the dazzling riches of the Shakespearian conceptions and style.

But bourgeois criticism, which does not deviate from the beaten path, maintained a low level in the case of Shakespeare. Sarcey wrote that the English poet irritated him and even Zola did not feel inclined to go into raptures over his works; Shakespeare and Victor Hugo bewildered him. But Zola, who at the beginning of Salvini's performance had exclaimed that he would leave Shakespeare in his glory because he could not understand him on the stage, especially in Italian before a public which becomes ecstatic over him, was at last carried away by the acting of the great Italian artist. Shyly coming out of his reserve the aged novelist wrote that in the Italian theatre he had experienced the most profound emotion he could remember. 'The Italian actor has completely gripped me; he has awakened my enthusiasm; I felt there was in him a living being moved by the same passions as myself. He presented the last moments of the dying man in *Hamlet* with such realism that he inspired the audience with terror.'

Later in France, as well as in Italy, there was such enthusiasm for Shakespeare that men began to devour his writings while his poetry was recited with the most sincere admiration. Victor Hugo as an old man, finally seeing all his efforts to popularise Shakespeare crowned with success, hailed Salvini with the mind of a poet and the heart of a citizen: 'All Paris', he wrote, 'applauds and admires you. Your interpretations of Shakespeare are soul-stirring. Italy whose fame is equal to her glory must needs be proud of you. France would be happy to account you as one of her own sons. A greater nationality unites us both, the Fatherland of Art, which is the World. The true public of a genius such as yours is Humanity. Take back to noble Italy the glory we have conferred on you, convey to her our admiration and enthusiasm and our wishes for your return to our midst.'

Shakespeare has gained the highest pinnacle of fame in dramatic art. He has had as interpreters the greatest artists of the stage; and the literary and dramatic critics of Europe have studied and analysed both the author and his actors. In the present century tragedy has been abandoned on almost all the stages of Europe. Artists no longer devote themselves to tragedy whether classical, romantic or historical. Society comedy has overflowed the stage and the inundation has destroyed the seeds which prudent and conscientious planters had sown in the fields of art. Nevertheless even to-day Shakespeare's works are more played on the Italian stage than in either France or Germany. All his tragedies offer a splendid field for Italian artists and they take full advantage of their opportunities. Hamlet, Othello, King Lear and Romeo seem to fascinate them; and to interpret these characters is the ambition of every young actor. Ermete Novelli, Gustavo Salvini, the son of the great actor, Ferruccio Garavaglia, Giovanni Grasso, Ermete Zacconi played all these parts.

Ermete Novelli was never equalled in the part of Petruchio. 'Those who heard him will never forget his voice,' wrote Addison MacLeod. 'Now roaring in frenzy, now crying in wrath, now pouring out in pity, now expanding in serene contemplation; without rising or sinking, increasing or diminishing, it seemed to become invested with a new moral quality, which in spite of the difference of language conveyed his meaning to the hearer. It was like an infinite organ whose many stops, changing at the will of a master intelligence, breathed out through the same pipes hate, love, triumph, sorrow, pity, contempt, arrogance, irritation, patient despair, unquenchable hope, infinite compassion; which at times sinking to a point when music seemed scarcely maintained in sound above the throes of silence, now swelled, now roared, now rose into magnificent harmony; whose variety composed into a passage uniform and tranquil, but yet full of inspiration; towering and tremulous with emotion and thought.

SHAKESPEARE ON THE ITALIAN STAGE

'The only other actor who had anything of this power was Sir Henry Irving and he was far behind Novelli. If I tried to follow Novelli through all the parts in which I have seen him I should lose myself. The best part for an English audience to see him in would undoubtedly be that of Louis XI because there he would challenge comparison with the greatest English actor within living memory. And great as Irving was in this part Novelli had just that natural ease which distinguishes the eagle from the flying machine. . . . In his Hamlet there were wonderful passages. His Play Scene was grand, and above all in the scene with the Ghost he made me feel the reality of the presence of a being from the other world. They say that in the presence of spirits animals cower and tremble though the cause of their fear is invisible to us. Something of this seemed to come into the actor's bearing. He did not cower or tremble but his whole being seemed touched into a sensibility not explicable by anything we saw or heard.'

Though Shakespeare does not appeal to modern Italian actresses Adelaide Ristori excelled as Lady Macbeth and Juliet, Emma Grammatica distinguished herself in *Much Ado About Nothing* and in *Measure for Measure* and Gina Favre in the rôle of Ophelia. Among more recent Italian Shakespearian actors we may mention Ruggero Ruggeri and Ettore Petrolini, both well known in England for they acted in various English theatres. Ruggeri has been compared to Sir Henry Irving. 'Strangely enough,' one dramatic critic wrote, 'having regard to Ruggeri's nationality his methods seem to have been modelled on those of Henry Irving. This is not intended to imply that he has deliberately imitated the style and methods of the English actor whom in all probability he never saw upon the stage. Nevertheless, one could not but be impressed by the similarity shown in their respective performances.'

Of all the Shakespearian plays *The Taming of the Shrew*, *Romeo and Juliet*, *King Lear*, *Othello* and *Hamlet* are most frequently acted with success on the Italian stage. The Compagnia Stabile of Rome presented *Julius Caesar* and *King Lear* at the Teatro Argentina, where some years ago *A Midsummer Night's Dream*, given for twenty-two evenings to a crowded house, initiated the most wonderful Shakespearian revival in Italy, which culminated with the imposing success of *Coriolanus* and *Julius Caesar* produced at the Costanzi Theatre in Rome by the gifted artist Gualtiero Tumiati and with an open-air performance of *The Merchant of Venice* staged in the City of the Doges in presence of a large number of illustrious Italians.

DID SHAKESPEARE KNOW ITALIAN?

It seems as if Shakespeare must somehow or other have learned enough Italian to read and understand our writers. *Dramatis personae*, like Mercutio for example, cannot avoid the Italian linguistic forms which Shakespeare employs with great ability and success. The greeting between Hortensio and Petruchio (*The Taming of the Shrew*, Act I, scene ii) is exchanged in two or three lines of pure Italian.

> *Pet.* Signior Hortensio, come you to part the fray?
> 'Con tutto il core, ben trovato', may I say.
> *Hor.* 'Alla nostra casa ben venuto, molto honorato signor mio, Petrucio.'

And Holofernes in *Love's Labour's Lost* quotes the well-known proverb:

> Venetia, Venetia,
> Chi non ti vede, non ti pretia.

Speaking of the merchant his use of the word 'pedant' in the sense of 'pedestrian' is analogous to that of our 'pedone', while this same 'pedant' declares that Tranio will always be the patron (i.e. *il padrone*) of his life and liberty. (*The Taming of the Shrew*, Act III, scene iv.) The word 'traghetto', used in Venice to signify an anchorage for gondolas, appears in the plays in the anglicised form of 'traject'. Frequently we find whole lines translated literally from Italian without the slightest alteration.

SHAKESPEARE AND ITALY

Mi perdonato, gentle master mine,

Basta; content thee, for I have it full,

and many other similar instances.

The majority of proverbs found in Shakespeare's plays are Italian or of Italian origin; as, for example, 'se fortuna mi tormenta, la speranza mi contenta'. In *The Two Gentlemen of Verona* we find, 'Sound as a fish,' 'sano come un pesce' being an expression still in common use in certain parts of Italy. Often Shakespeare's proverbs have given rise to protracted and futile discussions amongst critics who have little knowledge of Italian language and customs. This was exemplified some years ago by the correspondence in the columns of an English literary review on the subject of 'The Lady of the Strachy'. Shakespeare has a perfect knowledge of the correct use of names belonging to the Italian aristocracy of his own time; Lucentio, for example, describes his father Vincentio as 'come of the Bentivolii'. He is also acquainted with the dialectal forms of Christian names e.g. Petruccio, Francisco, Marianna, Caterina, Ortensio, Fidele; and he often amuses himself by playing on their significance in English.

The frequent use that the poet made of Italian *Novelle* and other works and the accuracy with which he introduced proper names and even whole sentences into his dramas are sufficient proof of the poet's knowledge of the Italian language. It has been argued that in Elizabethan England translations of Italian books abounded, but certainly Shakespeare's knowledge of

DID SHAKESPEARE KNOW ITALIAN?

life and customs in Italy was not entirely derived from them. In his lifetime some of the books to which he was indebted for much of his material had not been translated into English. In the collection of tales by Ser Giovanni Fiorentino entitled *Il Pecorone* we find the whole plot of the *Merchant of Venice*; and in the *Hecatomiti* of Cinthio we may read the story of *Othello*, and that of the adventures of Isabella, which Shakespeare utilised in *Measure for Measure*. Many of Cinthio's *Novelle* had been translated into French, but the tragic tale of Othello was to be found in neither French nor English. This collection of short stories—*Il Pecorone*—was only published in Italy in 1558, and in Shakespeare's time existed solely in the original. The simple story of the Jew and the pound of flesh might be traced to other sources, but only in *The Merchant of Venice* and in *Il Pecorone* do we find that the debtor, Antonio, whose pound of flesh was demanded by the creditor, is liberated by the skilful defence and intercession of the Lady of Belmont, wife of the debtor's own friend. In every other detail, too, we note that Shakespeare faithfully followed the Italian original, whose characters are transferred to the English comedy without the slightest alteration.

On reading *Hamlet* we feel that we are studying a work of a philosophical and scientific nature. Undoubtedly in the contemplative atmosphere of this drama we detect the preponderating influence exercised upon the poet by our philosopher, Giordano Bruno; an influence clearly recognisable, for example, in the soliloquy, 'To be, or not to be' and in some of the sonnets, notably Nos. 106, 109 and 123. It is true that Giordano Bruno had been for several years in England, had lectured at Oxford University and had been in London a guest of the French Ambassador, who had introduced him to the most influential people at Court, in particular to Sir Philip Sidney; but not a single work of his had been translated into English, not even *La Cena delle Ceneri*, in which he ridicules the habits of the Oxford dons. In *Hamlet* too Shakespeare introduced a purely Mantuan episode connected with the Court of the Gonzagas. The tale is written in choice Italian and our poet must undoubtedly have had recourse to MSS. in Italian.

In *Othello*, Act III, scenes iii and iv there are many reminiscences of Italian poets; and these references are of great interest, showing as they do not only the poet's learning but also the subjects of his studies. In Canto LI of Berni's revision of the *Orlando Innamorato* we find Iago's declaration:

> Who steals my purse steals trash; ...
> But he that filches from me my good name
> Robs me of that which not enriches him
> And makes me poor indeed.

Another reminder of Berni is to be found in Othello's farewell to military life:

> O, now for ever
> Farewell the tranquil mind! farewell content!
> Farewell! Othello's occupation's gone!

Indubitably Shakespeare derived material from Machiavelli's *Mandrangora* and he gives us the impression of knowing also *The Prince* and other works of the illustrious statesman, but for reasons of popularity he subscribes to the general belief in the historian's wickedness. As a contrast to Machiavel, the type of astute politician, he occasionally introduces Aretino as an example of the sensuality and corruption of the times.

The study of Ariosto in Italian has also left many traces in the plays of Shakespeare. In *Othello*, for instance, the language of the hero when he is speaking of the handkerchief:

> A sibyl
> In her prophetic fury sewed the work.

reminds us of a similar passage in Ariosto; and in writing *The Tempest* our dramatist must certainly have had in mind stanzas from Canto XLIII of the *Orlando Furioso*. Stanzas 14 and 15 especially contain something similar to the episode of Prospero and Miranda, while in stanza 187 allusion is made to the use of the magic arts in arousing or calming tempests. In the same play we find too that Shakespeare made use of the works of the Venetian explorer, Marco Polo. In *Much Ado About Nothing* our dramatist took the details for his plot from several Italian works. From the first canto of the *Furioso* (the story of Ariodante and Ginevra had already furnished the material for a drama presented at Court) he derived the idea of the malevolent lord trying to persuade a young lover of the infidelity of his beloved. Other details were taken from a *novella* of Bandello.

English critics have tried to minimise the importance of the fact that four-fifths of Elizabethan dramas were based on Italian *Novelle*. But these dramatists were indebted to the *Novellieri* for much more than the material for their tragedies and romantic comedies. The sight of such vivid pictures of a free and passionate life aroused the minds and excited the emotions of the phlegmatic English, making the blood course more vigorously through their veins. From a study of our *Novelle* their dramatists learned the vast and hitherto unknown possibilities of human existence which gave a new and powerful stimulus to their life. Moreover, these volumes of *Novelle* which had found their way into every household prepared the minds of the audience to receive sympathetically the performances of their own English tragedies and comedies. Between 1560 and 1590 there appeared in England more than fifteen collections of the *Novelle* translated from the Italian, many of them being reprinted several times. Thus it was that the Italian *Novelle* exercised a powerful and decisive influence upon that most characteristic product of the English Renaissance—the Elizabethan Drama.

It is important to add that Shakespeare's debt towards Italian literature is not confined to the *Novellieri* and other writers already mentioned. The technical apparatus and stage settings also originated in Italy; in fact, they were merely reproductions and imitations of the Italian stage as introduced by the actors of the Commedia dell'Arte. This and the Commedia Erudita have left profound traces upon all

DID SHAKESPEARE KNOW ITALIAN?

the poet's works, even on those whose spirit seems most remote from Italian art. Much has already been written on this subject, but we hope that some of the younger generation will devote themselves seriously to further research, in the excellent results of which they will doubtless find ample rewards.

Italian lyrical poetry has also played an important part in providing inspiration for his dramas, whilst in his sonnets Shakespeare has shown himself to be a worthy disciple of our neo-Platonic poets from Guido Guinizelli to Petrarch, and from Petrarch to Bembo, Michelangelo and Tasso. Nor was the poet ignorant of another field in which the Italians displayed their imaginative powers. In several passages he gives the impression of being well acquainted with particular works of our Renaissance painters and sculptors. In *The Winter's Tale* he speaks enthusiastically of his contemporary, Giulio Romano, and describes the supposed statue of Hermione as the one conceived by that remarkable Italian artist, who was the renowned and perfect imitator of natural beauty. Giulio Romano is better known as a painter than as a sculptor; but in the earlier part of his life he devoted himself to sculpture; and although here the name of Michelangelo might have been more appropriately cited, Shakespeare is not guilty of ignorance or carelessness in associating with the name of Giulio Romano the supreme qualities of Italian Renaissance sculpture.

DID SHAKESPEARE VISIT ITALY?

Is it possible that Shakespeare visited Italy? From the very start of his career the land of the Renaissance had exercised a great fascination over him, and the critics have rightly marvelled at the profound knowledge of the whole Italian peninsula which his plays reveal; but several whose scenes are laid in Italy have given rise to misconceptions and disputes. Italy with its public and private life, its laws and customs, its ceremonial and other characteristics, pulsates in every line of our dramatist, while the atmosphere of many scenes is Italian in the truest sense of the word. We cannot but wonder how Shakespeare obtained such accurate information, and we have no hesitation in affirming that on at least one occasion he must have visited Italy.

It may be asked, 'How and when could he have undertaken this journey?' *The Two Gentlemen of Verona* and *Romeo and Juliet* must be considered as his first declaration of love for Italy. Yet in these two plays we find little that encourages us to believe that the poet had actually seen the locality where the development of the action takes place. It is quite the contrary when we consider some of the later dramas, for example, *The Taming of the Shrew, The Merchant of Venice, Measure for Measure, Twelfth Night* and *Othello*, in all of which the scenes are purely Italian. Here we find such definite characteristics, such vivid local colour and such a wealth of precise and vigorous details that we are forced to conclude that Shakespeare must have visited Milan, Verona, Venice, Padua and Mantua. With this in mind we can fix with some certainty the date of his journey between the autumn of 1592 and the summer of 1593—the period when the Plague was so prevalent in his own country that, for fear of it, the sittings of the London Law Courts were suspended. At this time, too, the Queen prohibited all dramatic performances at Court, and the Council of State issued a proclamation forbidding any religious or political gatherings.

It was natural that a man of Shakespeare's culture and intellect should seize this opportunity of seeing for himself the beauties of Italy; because to the literary and artistic world of his day Italy was, as she had always been and always will be, the mother of learning and of classical culture. Men like Wyatt, Surrey, Sidney and Spenser studied her literature and imitated her poets; and, as Symonds declares, the example of Italy exerted an influence on every department of study and on every branch of intellectual activity. Three centuries in advance of all other countries in the fields of science and art, with names such as Dante, Petrarch, Boccaccio, Ariosto and Tasso amongst their classics, with a varied literature of tales, treatises, comedies, tragedies, pastoral and lyrical dramas, with the great histories of Machiavelli and Guicciardini, with their political philosophy and metaphysical research the Italians inevitably attracted men of taste in England, inspiring them to imitation and reproduction. Surrey and Wyatt brought back from Italy blank verse, the sonnet, the ottava rima, the sestina, etc.; Spenser wrote his *Faerie Queene* under the influence of Italian chivalrous poetry; Raleigh could not confer higher praise than to say that the reading of such verse would have made Petrarch shed tears of jealousy for his poetic fame, while Sidney copied the Italians in his lyrics and imitated Sannazzaro in his *Arcadia*.

Italy was the magic land where the joys of life abounded. With even the slenderest resources it was possible to undertake the pilgrimage, for one could travel at little expense on foot, on horseback, by boat or even in a carriage. Living in those days was very inexpensive—lodgings were obtainable for a few coppers at an inn or tavern, while the very poor could always find hospitality in the monasteries or colleges. All the most illustrious personages of the period had visited this glorious land; men of science like Latimer, Bacon and Harvey; poets and prose-writers like Lilly, Sidney, Nash and Greene; painters and sculptors, too, had sojourned there. Many of them have left us accounts of their travels, but if, with regard to Shakespeare, we possess no biographical information, we have at least many other important facts to adduce in support of our belief.

English critics while seeming to encourage the idea that Shakespeare was an unlearned genius fallen meteor-like from heaven, aver with strange inconsistency that it was easy enough for him to obtain the necessary information by consulting the volumes about travels in Italy which were in circulation at that time. They even go so far as to quote a long list of books in

DID SHAKESPEARE VISIT ITALY?

Italian, French, Latin, English and German—books which in all probability the dramatist never either saw or read. Some Italian authors have asserted that Shakespeare must have obtained information relating to Italy at the house of the Earl of Southampton, an Italianate Englishman whose court was frequented by the most celebrated literary men of the period, prominent amongst whom was Florio, a professor of Italian in London and Oxford, an able teacher and writer, who by his books and lectures had popularised Italian literature amongst the Elizabethan courtiers. It has even been suggested that Florio was in reality author of many of Shakespeare's dramas; but however flattering this conjecture may be to a teacher of Italian in Great Britain, it is a theory which we cannot accept because what Shakespeare knew of our country, of its customs and its life, was assuredly not derived from any of these sources.

The various scenes of *Othello* are no mere Venetian reminiscences, but pictures exhaling the very spirit of Venice, which Shakespeare has transferred to his drama. The darkness of morning, the narrow and mysterious 'calli', Brabantio's house with its heavy iron-barred doors, the Sagittary, the official residence of the commanders of the galleys, the hired gondolier witness of gallant intrigues, the gondola where the lovers had been seen, the galleys sent on a multitude of errands, the armaments, the attendants with torches, the special night guards, the council chamber, the senators, the Doge—the beloved Signor Magnifico—the discussions about the war, Brabantio's accusation that his daughter had been stolen and seduced by means of drugs and witchcraft, the history of Othello with all the sacrifices made in defence of the republic, the appearance of the divine Desdemona, fair and beautiful as a Titian portrait—all give the impression of a vivid portrayal of scenes enacted in the very heart of the Queen of the Adriatic.

The local colour of the *Taming of the Shrew* displays such an intimate acquaintance not only with the manners and customs of Italy but also with the minutest details of domestic life that it cannot have been gleaned from books or acquired in the course of conversations with travellers returned from Padua. The form of marriage between Petruchio and Katharine, which was later recommended by Manzoni's loquacious Agnese to Renzo and Lucia, was Italian and not English. Some lines where the noble lord proposes to show Sly his pictures:

> We'll show thee Io as she was a maid;
> And how she was beguiled and surprised,
> As lively painted as the deed was done.

suggest that the poet may have seen Correggio's famous picture—*Giove ed Io*—which is quite possible if he visited the north of Italy in 1592–3, because from 1585 to 1600 the picture was exhibited to the public in the palace of the sculptor, Leoni, in Milan, where it was admired by numerous travellers.

The description of Gremio's house and furnishings is striking because it represents an Italian villa of the sixteenth century with all its comforts and noble luxury.

DID SHAKESPEARE VISIT ITALY?

> My hangings all of Tyrian tapestry;
> In ivory coffers I have stuffed my crowns;
> In cypress chests my arras, counterpoints,
> Costly apparel, tents, and canopies,
> Fine linen, Turkey cushions boss'd with pearl,
> Valance of Venice gold in needlework,
> Pewter and brass, and all things that belong
> To house or housekeeping:

These magnificent *objets d'art* were only to be found in Italy, in the palaces of the aristocracy of Milan, Genoa, Turin, Pavia, etc. since living conditions in England were very primitive, and not even Elizabeth's courtiers could boast of possessing such refinements. In his *Cena delle Ceneri* Giordano Bruno speaks most disparagingly of the filth and coarseness of England, referring in particular to the disgusting table manners of her inhabitants. In *The Taming of the Shrew*, too, we find frequent references to the Alps, to Padua, to the River Po, to Venetian territory and to

> fruitful Lombardy,
> The pleasant garden of great Italy;

convincing evidence that the poet must have travelled in the country and brought back with him a clear recollection of its features.

In the *Merchant of Venice* we find an inimitable Italian atmosphere, whose fragrance can be more easily perceived than explained or analysed. The topography is so precise and accurate that it must convince even the most superficial reader that the poet visited the country, acutely observant of all its characteristics as he travelled through its mountains and valleys. One instance is the gift of a dish of pigeons which Gobbo takes to his son's master. Gobbo is a purely Venetian name, which must certainly have been suggested to Shakespeare by the statue of the kneeling hunchback of the Rialto, which forms the base of the pillar upon which in ancient days were affixed the decrees of the Republic. The scene where Portia despatches Balthasar in all haste by the common ferry on the River Brenta, which commanded the trade routes to Venice, cannot be sufficiently praised for its precision. We may conjecture that the country estate of Belmont, where the villa is situated, corresponds to our Monte Bello, and that Balthasar with the documents and Bellario's gown was to meet his mistress at the landing stage. Portia and Nerissa travel by carriage and, according to the poet, the distance they must traverse is twenty miles.

'For we must measure twenty miles to-day.'

The exact distance between Monte Bello and Padua is twenty miles; and this amazing accuracy is no chance coincidence.

But what gives the most characteristically Venetian flavour to this drama is the Rialto, around which the poet concentrates all his knowledge of the city of Venice. It is here that he wishes to transport his audience in imagination, that he would have us see the throng on the bridge and crowding the long flights of steps at either end of it. We can see the good Antonio going around with his friends in the hope of receiving news of his ships, and Shylock, slow and hesitating, fearing to attract the notice of the urchins, who never failed to torment the Jew whenever they chanced to recognise him. Amongst the *dramatis personae* also Venetian characteristics are faithfully sustained. Portia is a true Venetian lady, whilst Shylock and Antonio are indisputable types. The nature of the Jew, as represented by Shylock, would have been impossible in England, where the resettlement of the Jews had not yet been permitted after their expulsion. In Venice, on the other hand, there were in those days four or five thousand of them. Indeed Shylock in many respects represents the ordinary Venetian merchant; not a merchant such as Antonio, of course, for he is described as exceptional, but the typical city merchant who, in his methods and the conduct of his business, did not greatly differ from the Jew of popular imagination.

Italian lawyers and jurists of the Middle Ages and the Renaissance travelled round the cities of Italy putting their counsel and culture at the disposal of the public; very often they decided lawsuits and gave judgment in commercial and civil cases submitted to them. Our English dramatist gives us in *The Merchant of Venice* an example of this method of procedure; but for his convenience and to give more prominence to the love the rich Lady of Belmont bore to Bassanio, and her admiration for Antonio, he inverts the parts, making the noble lady play the part of judge in place of the jurist Bellario. There is just one instance where the Venetian tradition is violated—the characters of Launcelot Gobbo, the clown, and his old father. They are both peasants, but their actions, the tone of their conversation and their humour are not Italian. It is in Portia and Nerissa, Shylock and the Rialto that we enjoy the true Venetian aroma exhaled by the play.

THE GEOGRAPHY OF ITALY IN SHAKESPEARIAN DRAMA

Notwithstanding the fact that his Italian scenes are depicted in colours faithfully reproduced from the originals, the majority of commentators tell us that Shakespeare knew nothing of conditions in northern Italy, and that he was totally ignorant of the geography of these provinces. Three well-known passages are quoted in support of their assertion: the first in *The Tempest*, the second in *The Two Gentlemen of Verona* and the third in *The Taming of the Shrew*. Sidney Lee, our dramatist's biographer, never tires of reiterating this argument to prove Shakespeare guilty of saying things which in fact he neither said nor thought. It is erroneously repeated that Shakespeare described Verona as a city on the sea coast, and Bergamo as a place where canvas was woven for the making of sails, without considering that Shakespeare in his allusions to Verona was careful to mention not the sea but the very river—the Adige—which flows through that city; and that if he asserts that Tranio's father followed the trade of sail-maker in Bergamo he cannot have been far from the truth, for the city of Bergamo has been famous for that industry until recent times. Indeed, Manzoni, in his *I Promessi Sposi*, describing the flight of Renzo, speaks of the sail-making industry which flourished in that district. But perhaps it will be better to give here some further examples to illustrate our argument. In

The Tempest, Prospero relates how he had been taken out of the gates of Milan, put upon a ship and despatched some leagues to the sea. The poet's sole error here is in making the voyage too short; but even this is explained in the line,

> 'In few, they hurried us aboard a bark.'

The words 'in few' indicate that he has much else to say and cannot waste time on useless descriptions. 'In few' corresponds to the Italian *'in breve'*, which is sufficiently significant. In those days it was quite possible to embark at the gates of Milan for ports on the Adriatic Sea, and since, in the sixteenth century, there were no railways, a journey by water was often preferable to one by road because of its greater safety and comfort.

But if Shakespeare is to be accused of inexactitude what shall we say of other writers: Goldoni, for instance, who in his *Memoirs* describes at length a voyage which he made, in company with a Dominican Friar, from Pavia to Chioggia? Montaigne, Coryat and others tell us that in their wanderings from one city to another in northern Italy they were in the habit of travelling by boat. In *The Two Gentlemen of Verona* Shakespeare describes Valentine as sailing from Verona to Milan. This is another passage quoted by critics to prove that Shakespeare's information was not the result of personal observation; but here also the accusation of ignorance is wholly unjustified. In *Romeo and Juliet* the city of Verona has no harbour and is said to be situated in the midst of the Venetian Plain, as in reality it is. From a superficial reading of *The Two Gentlemen of*

Verona one might think that the city was on the coast, since the word 'road' is used for the place of Valentine's embarkation, and several allusions are made to the ebb and flow of the tide. But such expressions do not necessarily indicate that the city was a seaport. It is true that 'road' is now only used of the sea, but in the sixteenth century and even much later it merely signified a place where large ships could be anchored. Hundreds of examples from English authors prove that Shakespeare did not err, for the word is freely used in descriptions of towns on the River Thames. As for the ebb and flow of the waves, it is well known that the effects of the tide can be seen more than a hundred miles from the mouth of a river.

But all these discussions seem of little consequence when we read the drama more diligently and ponder carefully the words of the poet, who, at the end of his description of the journey by water, speaks not of the sea but of the river:

> 'Tut, man, I mean thou'lt lose the flood, and, in losing the flood, lose thy voyage, and, in losing thy voyage, . . .'

The reply to this apostrophe which has been overlooked by commentators proves the dramatist to have been more accurate than he has generally been given credit for.

> 'Lose the tide, and the voyage, and the master, and the service, and the tied! Why, man, if the river were dry, I am able to fill it with my tears; if the wind were down, I could drive the boat with my sighs.'

'If the river were dry'—what is this river? Without doubt the Adige, on whose banks Verona was built, a river which in the sixteenth century had communications with many of the cities of northern Italy, including Milan. The River Adige which comes from the direction of Milan and flows through Verona was a navigable river; and Milan itself was situated on several canals, by means of which it was possible to travel from city to city. Three administrators were appointed by the Venetian Republic to supervise commerce on the River Adige and these canals. Verona appears to have been a port of some consequence, often visited by the galleys of the Republic of St. Mark, stationed in Lake Garda a few miles from the city. It seems as if critics wish to judge Shakespeare by twentieth-century conditions, forgetting that journeys on foot or by coach in earlier centuries, and especially in the time of Shakespeare, were neither comfortable nor safe. Therefore all the rivers and canals of northern Italy were utilised for commerce and travel, these means of communication playing an important part in the history of Italy long before *The Tempest* or *The Two Gentlemen of Verona* were written or published. We have chronicles, letters, and numerous documents of merchants, diplomatists and historians in which they are mentioned; and it is impossible to write the history of Venetian commerce and of the Galleys of the Republic without giving prominence to their usefulness both in peace and war.

The River Po, with its thirty main tributaries and many smaller ones, was in the fifteenth and sixteenth centuries, as in earlier times, the principal means of transport for the inhabitants of northern Italy; and one cannot read the history of its cities without noting the numerous allusions to the commerce carried on by these waterways. Even Polibius tells us that the river was navigable for 250 miles from the sea; Straboni speaks of Roman navigation from Piacenza to Ravenna, and Pliny alludes to the trading ships which sailed up the Po to the place where Turin now stands. From the twelfth century onwards the Po and its tributaries became still more important. Italian chroniclers assert that Milan in the fourteenth century enjoyed all the advantages that were to be gained through the possession of a canal which communicated with the Po, and that later, for the transport of the marble which was to be used in building the Duomo, the city constructed other canals leading to the Ticino, the Po and to Lake Maggiore. All this justifies Carlo Pagano's assertion in 1520 that Milan, though far from the sea, might easily be reckoned a seaport. English travellers mention that many of their compatriots travelled by boat down the Po from Turin to Venice. Coryat speaking of Milan declares that the city was surrounded by a network of canals whose waters flowed into the river.

When we come to consider the aspect presented by the Adige and Po in time of war, the amount of traffic along their courses is nothing less than marvellous and a source of astonishment to those who doubt the possibility of a voyage from Milan to the sea. The historian Guicciardini writes that in 1509 the Po was the scene of bitter naval battles between the galleys of Milan and Venice. We may add that in 1431 Niccolò Trevisano, an Admiral of the Venetian Republic, had his fleet destroyed by the Milanese, under the command of

Ambrogio Spinola, not far from Cremona. This was a serious blow for the Venetians, who lost no time in building a powerful fleet to humiliate the proud Duke of Milan and the Marquis of Mantua. In August, 1438, a fleet of a hundred galleons, thirty barques, six galleys and many other vessels loaded with provisions and munitions sailed up the Po from Venice to attack the region of Milan.

Shakespeare's accurate knowledge of the geography of Italy is all the more noteworthy as it contrasts strikingly with his ignorance of that of other European countries, France, for example. In his allusions to French towns we find nothing to indicate that he knew them well. In the three plays of which the scenes are laid in France—*Love's Labour's Lost, As You Like It* and *All's Well That Ends Well*—local colour and topographical realism are entirely absent. The scene is for the most part set in districts far removed from the direct route to Italy; but all the cities where a traveller on his way to Italy would stop to change horses or coaches are accurately named by our dramatist, e.g. Calais, Amiens, Longueville, Troyes, Marseilles and Genoa. When we consider that in the north of Italy he reveals a more profound knowledge of Milan, Bergamo, Verona, Mantua, Padua and Venice, the very limitation of the poet's notions of geography proves that he derived his information from an actual journey through Italy and not from books. All that he says about our country is marvellously accurate, and this precision is manifest not only in the passages already cited but in all those adduced by the critics to prove his ignorance of the geography of Italy. A German critic asserted that he could not have known Padua and Venice because in *The Merchant of Venice* he describes these two cities as 'neighbouring'. Since Padua is only about twenty miles from Venice one can hardly deny the proximity of the two cities. A statement such as Shakespeare's, besides being correct to-day, seems all the more exact when one remembers that he wrote it towards the end of the sixteenth century.

Another critic based his accusation of ignorance on the fact that Shakespeare had alluded in *The Two Gentlemen of Verona* to a forest in the Province of Milan, extending in the direction of Bergamo, where robbers had taken refuge. If Shakespeare is in error here, then so too is Manzoni, who describes the Gran Macchia into which Renzo plunged on the night of his flight from Milan to the territory of St. Mark. Here too Shakespeare is correct, because he places the forest in the only locality where it ever existed or could have existed. Still another writer accuses Shakespeare of ignorance because in one of his plays he alludes to a small island in the River Po. This argument seems superficial and ridiculous when one thinks that, in reality, small pieces of land surrounded by water and called *isolotti* are by no means rare in the rivers and lakes of north Italy. It will suffice to mention the famous island of Belvedere, formed by the Po not far from Ferrara, where the Este family in the sixteenth century built a magnificent palace, and the *isolotti* on the Piave, of which so much was heard during the last phase of the fighting against the Austrians in 1918.

Thus all these arguments fail to prove Shakespeare's ignorance of the geography of Italy. Apart from a few trifling errors, the topographical details of the Italian cities with all their individual characteristics are surprisingly accurate in his plays: far more exact than in the works of many other writers who have visited Italy. Even Byron who travelled map in hand through Europe, and who earned such unstinted praise for the fidelity of his descriptions, made a considerable number of errors in his *Childe Harold*; Walter Scott, who knew Edinburgh as the Romans know their own city, made some unpardonable mistakes in his novel, *The Antiquary*; Chaucer, who made at least three journeys to Italy, in the Prologue to his *Clerkes Tale* makes the River Po flow beyond Venice; and of Browning, who loved and lived in Italy, one could cite many instances of errors in the description of scenes often visited and admired. But no one would dream of suggesting that Scott had never been in Edinburgh or that Chaucer and Browning had never visited Italy.

In conclusion we may affirm that of all the English poets who visited Italy, with the possible exception of Shelley and Byron, no one has depicted our scenes, our life, our character and our nature better than Shakespeare. The portrayer of the spirit of humanity, the genius of the English Renaissance, in whose works we find not only true life and passion, but all European institutions with their chivalry, courtesy and ambitions, could not have sung the praises of the classical yet ever romantic land of Italy without having paid her at least a fleeting visit. It need occasion no surprise therefore if we imagine the great lover of our country travelling through many Lombardian and Venetian cities 'waving friendly together the British and the Italian flag, and talking of the Alps, the Apennines and the River Po'. These words of the dramatist proved truly prophetic, for the Anglo-Italian flags waved victoriously together in the Crimea, in Sicily on Garibaldi's disembarkation in 1859 and on the sacred battlefields of more recent wars for the defence of that civilisation which is the glory of the Latin peoples.

INDEX

Aconzio, Jacopo, 61
Addison, 78
Adige, River, 141, 143, 145
Adriano di Castello, 54
Adriatic Sea, 142
Aeneid, 94
Algarotti, 101
Alighieri (see Dante)
All's Well That Ends Well, 96, 146
Amiens, 146
Aminta, 67
Amours de Voyage, 80
Andrea del Sarto, 83
Andrew, Archdeacon, 51
Anselm, 50
The Antiquary, 148
Apology for Poetrie, 66
Aquinas, Thomas, 34
Arcadia, 134
Architecture, 47, 71, 72, 73, 76, 79, 80
Aretino, 129
Ariosto, 39, 42, 67, 70, 74, 77, 129, 133
Aristodemo, 105
Aristotle, 34, 42, 66, 100
Arnold, M., 54
Ars Amandi, 94
Art, Celtic, 51
Art, Italian, 29, 47, 59, 64, 65, 67, 71, 73, 78, 79, 80, 81, 131, 136
Art, Greek, 40
Art, Roman, 40
Art of English Poesie, 66
Ascham, 57
Asolani, 66
As You Like It, 146
Athens, 93
Avignon, 12, 53

Bacon, Francis, 64, 65, 67, 89, 134
Bacon, Roger, 53
Ballet, 109
Bandello, 129
Banking, 62, 63, 64
Bardi, 62, 63
Baretti, 101, 102, 103, 104
Beaumont, 68
Becket, St. Thomas, 50
Beerbohm Tree, 119
Belvedere, Island of, 147
Bembo, Cardinal, 66, 111, 131
Benedictine Order, 51
Bentivoglio, 65
Beppo, 82
Bergamo, 141, 146, 147
Bernardi, 72
Bernhardt, Sarah, 118
Berni, 68, 77, 128
Bettinelli, 104, 105, 106
Bianchi, Celestino, 115
Blake, 78
Boccaccio, 39, 43, 53, 60, 70, 133
Boccalini, 68
Bobbio, Monastery of, 51
Boiardo, 60, 67
Bologna, 43, 50
Book of Polite Conversation, 66
Borgias, The, 60
Botticelli, 67
Bracciolini, Poggio, 55
Bramante, 73
Browning, Robert, 25, 44, 80, 83, 89, 115, 148
Browning, E. B., 43, 80, 82
Bruno, Giordano, 66, 127, 128, 137
Buckingham, Duke of, 99
Bucknell, 91
Burne-Jones, 78

INDEX

Byron, 31, 44, 80, 81, 82, 89, 148

Cabots, The, 64, 65
Calais, 147
Calvinism, 76
Cambridge, 15, 47, 54, 72, 76
Campanella, 66
Canova, 73
Canterbury, Archbishops of, 50
Canterbury Tales, 53, 148
Canzoniere, Il, 67
Capua, 50
Carbonari, 82
Carducci, 34, 43, 53, 95, 104
Carew, 70
Carlyle, 39
Carmeliana, Alice, 71
Carmeliano, Pietro, 54
Carne, Sir Edward, 56
Caruso, 108
Casa Guidi Windows, 82
Castelvetro, 66
Castiglione, 66, 68
Cato, 100
Cavallari, 71
Cazzola, Clementina, 108, 112, 114
Cellini, Benvenuto, 71
Cena delle Ceneri, La, 128, 137
Cesarotti, 104, 105, 106
Chaucer, 31, 39, 43, 45, 53, 60, 62, 79, 148
Chaucerians, Scottish, 53
Cherubini, Antonio, 109
Chiarini, 53
Chichester, 72
Chigi, 62
Childe Harold, 80, 148
Chioggia, 142
Church, Anglican, 61, 75, 76
Church, Roman, 48, 61, 76
Cicero, 40
Cinna, 103
Cinthio, 127
Cisalpino di Padua, 92
Clerico, Francesco, 109

Clerk, John, 56
Clorinda and Damon, 70
Clough, 43, 80
Coleridge, 79
Colet, 55, 60
Columbus, 64, 65
Comedy of Errors, The, 94, 96
Commedia dell'Arte, 31, 65, 130
Commedia Erudita, 65, 130
Commerce, 61, 62, 63, 64, 98
Comus, 74
Conti, Antonio, 99, 100
Coriolanus, 109, 112, 118, 120, 124
Corneille, 43, 100, 102, 103
Correggio, 78, 136
Cortegiano, Il, 66
Coryat, 58, 142, 145
Council of Trent, 75
Counter-Reformation, 75
Cranmer, 61
Crashaw, 68, 69, 70
Cremona, 146
Croce, 39
Cromwell, Oliver, 62
Cromwell, Thomas, 65
Cyder, 99
Cymbeline, 96

D'Annunzio, 18, 95
Dante, 31, 34, 35, 39, 41, 42, 53, 54, 55, 60, 67, 70, 74, 80, 88, 95, 97, 98, 106, 110, 111, 118, 133
Da Ponte, 109
Defence of Poetry, 66
Defoe, 64
De Gamerra, 104
De Joanne Cassiano, 17
Della Casa, 66, 111
De Luci Acci Vita et Scriptis, 17
Demosthenes, 40
Derby, Lord, 63
Description of England, 54
De Vulgari Eloquentia, 41
Diderot, 43
Diodati, Carlo, 74

152

INDEX

Divine Comedy, The, 31, 35, 54, 81
Doge, The, 63, 135
Dolce Favella, La, 18
Donatus, Bishop, 51
Donne, 68, 70
Dorset, 67
Douglas, 59
Dryden, 39, 43, 69, 78, 102
Due Spettri al Convito, I, 109
Dunbar, William, 53, 59

Eco dell'Ofanto, 13
Edinburgh, University of, 18
Edward III, 63
Electra, 93
Elizabethan Age, The, 41, 64, 65, 66, 68, 69, 70, 73, 87–149
English schools, 52
Epic Poetry of European Nations, 100
Erasmus, 60
Essay on Criticism, 66
Este family, 147
Eton College, 75
Euphuism, 70
Example of Virtue, 59

Faerie Queene, The, 134
Falstaff (Salieri), 109
Falstaff (Verdi), 109
Fanfani, Pietro, 111
Fascism, 20, 21, 34
Fasti, 94
Favre, Gina, 123
Fenton, Sir George, 66
Ferrara, 98, 147
Fiesole, 51
Filelfo, 56, 66
Filobiblion, 53
Fiorentino, Ser Giovanni, 127
Flaxman, 78
Fletcher, 68
Flodden, Battle of, 54
Florence, 15, 43, 44, 55, 61, 62, 64, 77, 80, 83, 89, 96, 98, 109, 111, 114
Florio, Angelo, 61

Florio, Giovanni, 61, 89, 135
Fogazzaro, 18
Folengo, 60, 68
Forbes-Robertson, 119
Fracastoro, 95
Fra Lippo Lippi, 83
Franciscans, 52, 53
Frescobaldi, 62
Friar Ochimo, 61
Frusta, La, 102

Gainsborough, 73, 78
Galateo, 66
Galilei, Galileo, 67, 77
Gamba, Pietro, 82
Garavaglia, Ferruccio, 122
Garda, Lake, 144
Garibaldi, 45, 149
Garnett, Dr., 61
Gautier, Théophile, 120
Gemme e Fiori, 18
Genoa, 45, 51, 98, 137, 146
George V, King, 47
Gerusalemme Liberata, 76
Ghirlandaio, 72
Gigli, Girolamo, 55
Giorgione, 67
Giove ed Io, 136
Gladstone, 45
Glasgow, University of, 15, 16, 18, 30, 31, 52, 60
Gloucester, Duke of, 55
Goldoni, 110, 142
Goldsmith, 78
Gonzagas, Court of the, 128
Gower, 53
Grafton, 65
Grammar, New Italian, 18
Grammatica, Emma, 123
Gran Macchia, 147
Grasso, Giovanni, 122
Gravina, 77
Gray, 79, 80
Greek, Shakespeare's Knowledge of, 93

153

INDEX

Greene, 67, 134
Grillo family, 11, 12, 13, 14
Grocyn, 55, 60
Grosseteste, Bishop, 53
Guarini, 67
Guazzo, 66
Guicciardini, 65, 67, 133, 145
Guidotti, 62
Guilty Mother, The, 104
Guinizelli, 18, 131

Halifax, Lord, 78
Hall, 65
Hallam, 69
Hamlet, 65, 91, 93, 94, 99, 103, 108, 109, 111, 112, 115–124, 127, 128
Hampton Court, 72
Harvey, 67, 92, 134
Hatton, Sir Christopher, 59
Hawes, Stephen, 59
Hecatomiti, 127
Henry IV, 93, 100
Henry VII, 51, 54, 62, 65, 71
Henry VIII, 45, 55, 56, 62, 65, 71
Henryson, Robert, 53, 59
Herbert, 68, 70
Herrick, 69, 70
Heywood, 56
Hogarth, 73, 78
Holinshed, 65
Homer, 40, 88, 102
Horace, 40, 95
Hugo, Victor, 120, 121
Hull, Edward, 59
Humphry Clinker, 44

Illuminati, 100
Il Penseroso, 74
Imaginary Conversations, 80
Insanity, Treatment of, 91
Irving, Sir Henry, 115–119, 123, 124
Italian Poets, 18
Italian Prose Writers, 18

James IV of Scotland, 54
Johnson, Dr., 70, 78, 101, 104

Jones, Inigo, 73
Julius Caesar, 49
Julius Caesar, 100, 104, 106, 112, 124
Juvenal, 95

Kean, Charles, 112, 119
Kean, Edmund, 115, 118, 119
Keats, 43, 80, 81
Kepler, 92
King Lear, 91, 103, 112, 118, 120, 122, 124
Knox, John, 61

Lady of the Strachy, 32, 126
La Fontaine, 43
L'Allegro, 74
Landor, 43, 80
Lanfranc, 50
Langland, John, 53
Latimer, 57, 60, 134
Law, Shakespeare's Knowledge of, 90, 139
Lee, Sidney, 141
Leghorn, 44
Leigh Hunt, 44, 80
Leonardo, 71
Leoncavallo, 109
Leoni, 136
Leopardi, 31, 95
Leopardi (bankers), 63
Lessing, 104
Leti, Gregorio, 99
Lettres Philosophiques, 99
Lewes, 118
Lilly, George, 56
Lilly, William, 56
Linacre, 55, 57, 60
Lincoln, 72
Lindsay, Sir David, 53
Literature, Comparative, 11, 19, 31, 34, 39
Literature, English, 19, 25, 31, 34, 39, 43, 52, 60, 62, 64, 66, 82, 102, 103

INDEX

Literature, European, 19, 39, 40, 42, 66, 101, 121
Literature, French, 43, 78, 101–106, 127
Literature, German, 43, 102, 103
Literature, Greek, 42, 93, 95, 102
Literature, Italian, 11, 17, 29, 31, 41, 56, 59, 60, 65–68, 73, 74, 82, 95, 96, 99, 101, 102, 104–106, 126, 128–131, 133–135
Literature, Latin, 42, 93–95, 102
Lombardi, 109
Lombardy, 61
London, 25, 55, 61, 66, 72, 78, 89, 96, 112, 115, 118, 128
Longueville, 146
Lope de Vega, 104
Lovelace, 70
Love's Labour's Lost, 94, 95, 125, 146
Lucca, 45, 50
Luther, 41
Lydgate, John, 3

'Macaronic' verse, 59
Macbeth, 65, 100, 109. 112, 120, 123
Machiavelli, 42, 65, 67, 128, 129, 133
MacLeod, Addison, 122
Maffei, 99
Maggiore, Lake, 145
Maiano, Giovanni da, 72
Mandrangora, 128
Mantua, 98, 128, 133, 146
Mantuano, Battista, 95
Manzoni, 106, 136, 141, 147
Marini, 69, 70, 74
Marlowe, 67, 68
Marrochesi, 109
Marseilles, 146
Marsilio, Ficino, 68
Marsilius of Padua, 60
Marvell, 69
Masques, 59
Mazzini, 39, 81
Measure for Measure, 96, 123, 127, 132

Medical Jurisprudence, 91
Medici, Lorenzo, 60, 62, 67
Megalotti, 99
Memoirs, Goldoni's, 142
Menander, 40
Mercatores Tusciae, 62
Merchant of Venice, The, 96, 112, 124, 127, 132, 137–140, 147
Mercurius, 106
Meredith, 80
Merope, 99
Merry Wives of Windsor, The, 94, 96
Metamorphoses, 93, 94
Metastasio, 104
Michelangelo, 131
Middle Ages, 41, 49–53, 58, 139
Midsummer Night's Dream, A, 124
Milan, 44, 51, 98, 109, 110, 112, 133, 136, 137, 142, 144–147
Millais, 73, 78
Milton, 34, 39, 43–45, 61, 67, 74–77, 79, 89
Milton, Life of, 100
Minturno, 66
Modena, Giovanni da, 72
Modena, Gustavo, 109–111
Molière, 43, 88, 103
Monmouth, Earl of, 66
Monnier, 42
Montaigne, 61, 89, 142
Monte Cassino, 12, 50
Monteverde, 77
Monti, 105, 108, 109
More, Sir T., 64
Morgante Maggiore, 82
Much Ado About Nothing, 96, 123, 129
Muratori, 77
Museum, British, 17, 25
Music, 27, 47, 59, 77–79

Naples, 45, 50, 77, 98
Nash, Thomas, 90, 134
Newton, 92

INDEX

Niccolini, 106
Normanby, Lord, 115
Novelle, 43, 68, 70, 126, 127, 129, 130
Novelli, Ermete, 108, 110, 122, 123
Nuova Atlantis, 64

Opera, 109, 118
Orator, Public, 54
Orfeo, 67
Orlando Furioso, 129
Orlando Innamorato, 128
Othello, 96, 103, 109-114, 117-120, 122, 124, 127-129, 132, 135, 136
Ovid, 93, 94
Oxford, 54-57, 66, 89, 128
Oxford Movement, 79

Padua, 43, 44, 56, 57, 61, 66, 97, 98, 108, 133, 136, 137, 146, 147
Padua, Giovanni da, 72
Pagano, Carlo, 145
Palestrina, 77
Palladio, 73
Pallavicini, 62
Paradise Lost, 44, 61, 74, 77
Paradise Regained, 74
Paradisi, 104
Paris, 120
Pastime of Pleasure, 59
Pastor Fido, 61
Pater, W., 80
Patti, Adelina, 118
Pavia, 43, 50, 137, 142
Pecorone, Il, 127
Pellico, 106
Perugia, 18, 19, 34
Peruzzi, 62, 63
Petrarch, 34, 39, 42, 53, 55, 60, 70, 74, 77, 95, 131, 133, 134
Petrolini, Ettore, 123
Philips, John, 99
Piacenza, 145
Piave, River, 147
Piccinini, 111, 112

Piccolomini, Cardinal Enea, 55
Pico della Mirandola, 68
Pignotti, 104
Piozzi, Mrs., 108
Pisa, 44, 61, 80, 82, 98
Plague, The Great, 133
Plautus, 40, 42, 94
Pléiade Française, 41
Pliny, 145
Plutarch, 95
Po, River, 137, 144-146, 147-149
Poetic Licence, 95
Poggio, 66
Pole, Cardinal R., 57
Polibius, 145
Politian, 55-57, 60, 67
Polo, Marco, 64, 65, 129
Pope, Alex., 39, 66, 69, 78, 104
Pope Alexander VI, 54
Pope Gregory XIII, 57
Pope John XXII, 53
Pope Nicholas V, 60
Pope Pius II, 60
Pope Urban VI, 12
Pre-Raphaelitism, 79
Primavera, 73
Prince, The, 129
Promessi Sposi, I, 136, 141, 147
Proverbs, 126
Pulci, 60, 67, 82
Puritanism, 58, 73, 78
Puttenham, 66

Quadrio, 101
Quarant' Anni di Vita Artistica, 112
Quiller-Couch, 47

Rabelais, 60
Rachel, 119
Racine, 103, 106
Raleigh, Prof. W., 54
Raleigh, Sir W., 134
Ramsay, Allan, 68
Rape of Lucrece, 67, 94
Raphael, 67, 104

INDEX

Ravenna, 44, 82, 145
Reformation, 41, 42, 56, 60, 61, 73, 74
Religion, 49–51, 56
Renaissance, 40, 41, 52, 56, 60, 64, 65, 66, 68–70, 73, 94–96, 110, 130–132, 148
Reynolds, Sir Joshua, 73, 78
Richard II, 112
Richard III, 100, 105
Richard of Bury, 53
Risorgimento, 45, 81
Ristori, Adelaide, 108, 123
Robinson Crusoe, 64
Rolli, Paolo, 99, 100
Roman Breviary, 50
Roman Empire, 45, 48, 49
Roman Missionaries and Ecclesiastics, 50
Roman Occupation, 12, 45–49
Romano, Giulio, 131
Romantic Revival, 79
Rome, 40, 43, 47, 48, 50, 51, 55–58, 64, 77, 81, 82, 96, 98, 113, 114, 124
Romeo and Juliet, 94, 96, 108, 109, 112, 122–124, 132, 142
Romney, 73
Rossetti, 73, 78, 81
Rossi, Ernesto, 108, 112
Rossini, 109, 110
Rousseau, 43
Ruggeri, Ruggero, 123
Ruskin, J., 45, 54, 80, 81

S. Angelo dei Lombardi, 11, 14, 20, 23, 24, 30
St. Augustine, 50
St. Bride, 51
St. Catherine of Siena, 60
St. Columbanus, 51
S. Filippo Neri, 77
St. Francis, 18
St. Paul, 48
St. Thomas Aquinas, 34

Sachs, Hans, 43
Saint Victor, Paul de, 120
Salieri, 109
Salvini, Gustavo, 122
Salvini, Tommaso, 108, 110, 112–121
Samson Agonistes, 74
Sannazzaro, 95, 134
Satan's Stratagems, 61
Savonarola, 60
Schiller, 110
Scientific Knowledge, Shakespeare's, 91, 92
Scott, Clement, 118
Scott, Sir Walter, 148
Secentism, 69, 70
Segni, 65
Seneca, 40, 42, 48, 95
Severino, S., 109
Severus, Emperor, 48
Sextiad, 67
Shakespeare, 31, 43, 44, 46, 61, 65, 67, 68, 70, 79, 87–149
Shakespeare and the Art of Printing, 90
Shakespeare and the Bible, 91
Shakespearian Myth, 91
Shelley, 31, 34, 43, 44, 66, 68, 80, 81, 148
Sidney, Sir P., 66, 67, 70, 128, 133, 134
Siena, 60, 61, 98
Skelton, 59
Smollett, T., 44
Somerset, Duke of, 72
Sophocles, 93
Southampton, 61, 63
Southampton, Earl of, 135
Spectator, The, 78
Spenser, 39, 43, 66–68, 70, 89, 102, 133, 134
Spezia, 44
Spinola, Ambrogio, 146
Steno, Niels, 92
Stevenson, R. L., 64

INDEX

Stow, 65
Straboni, 145
Studî Drammatici, 112
Surrey, 59, 60, 66, 67, 133
Swinburne, 80, 81
Symonds, 133

Taming of the Shrew, The, 94, 96, 124, 125, 132, 136, 137, 141
Tasso, 12, 39, 42, 67, 74, 75, 77, 131, 133
Teatro Argentina, 124
Teatro Borgognissanti, 109
Teatro Costanzi, 124
Teatro del Re, 110
Teatro S. Crisostomo, 108
Teatro Niccolini, 114
Telesio, 66
Tempest, The, 96, 100, 103, 129, 141, 142, 144
Tennyson, 89
Terence, 40, 95
Theatre, Blackfriars, 69
Theatre, Drury Lane, 117
Theatre, Globe, 69
Theatre, Haymarket, 99
Theatre, Italian (Paris), 120
Theatre, Lyceum, 115-118
Ticino, River, 145
Tintoretto, 67
Titian, 67, 136
Tombe di Verona, 109
Tomb of the English Poet, The, 104
Torrigiano, Pietro, 71, 72
Toto, 71
Tragedia Veronese, 108
Trajan, Emperor, 48
Treasure Island, 64
Trevisano, Admiral, 145
Trezzo, 73
Trissino, 66
Troilus and Cressida, 92
Troyes, 146
Tumiati, Gualtiero, 124
Turin, 112, 137, 145

Turner, 78
Twelfth Night, 32, 96, 132
Two Gentlemen of Verona, The, 96, 126, 132, 141, 142, 144, 147

Ubaldini (bankers), 62
Ubaldini (painter), 73
Umbria, 61
Unities, The, 100, 104
Universities, English, 15, 47, 54-57, 76, 89, 128
Universities, Italian, 15, 43, 52, 56, 58, 61
Universities, Scottish, 15, 16, 18, 30, 31, 52, 60
Urbino, 15
U.S.A., 19, 48
Utopia, 64

Valentini, 104
Valla, 60
Vallombrosa, 44
Varchi, 65
Vaughan, 68
Vecchi, 77
Venice, 44, 61, 63, 64, 77, 82, 96, 98, 109, 110, 112, 113, 124, 125, 129, 133, 135-140, 142, 144-149
Venus and Adonis, 67, 94
Vercelli, 50
Verdi, 109
Vermigli, Pietro Martire, 60
Verona, 98, 133, 141-144, 146
Veronese, Guarino, 55, 56
Veronese, Paolo, 67
Vespucci, Amerigo, 64, 65
Vicenza, 112, 113
Vida, 39, 66, 95
Vienna, 109
Vigano, Salvatore, 109
Villani, 63
Virgil, 40, 48, 88, 94
Virgilio, Polidoro, 55
Vita Nuova, La, 67
Vitelli, Cornelio, 54

INDEX

Vittorino da Feltre, 56
Volpe, 71
Voltaire, 42, 43, 99–103, 105, 106, 110

Warton, 79, 80
Watts, G. F., 78
Webster, 68
Wilson Barrett, 119
Windsor Castle, 62, 72
Winter's Tale, The, 131
Wolsey, Cardinal, 72

Words, Italian, 59, 62
Wordsworth, Bishop, 91
Wotton, Sir Henry, 75
Wren, Christopher, 73
Wyatt, 59, 60, 67, 133

Young, Dr., 71

Zacconi, Ermete, 108, 110, 122
Zeno, Apostolo, 99
Zola, 120
Zuccaro, 73

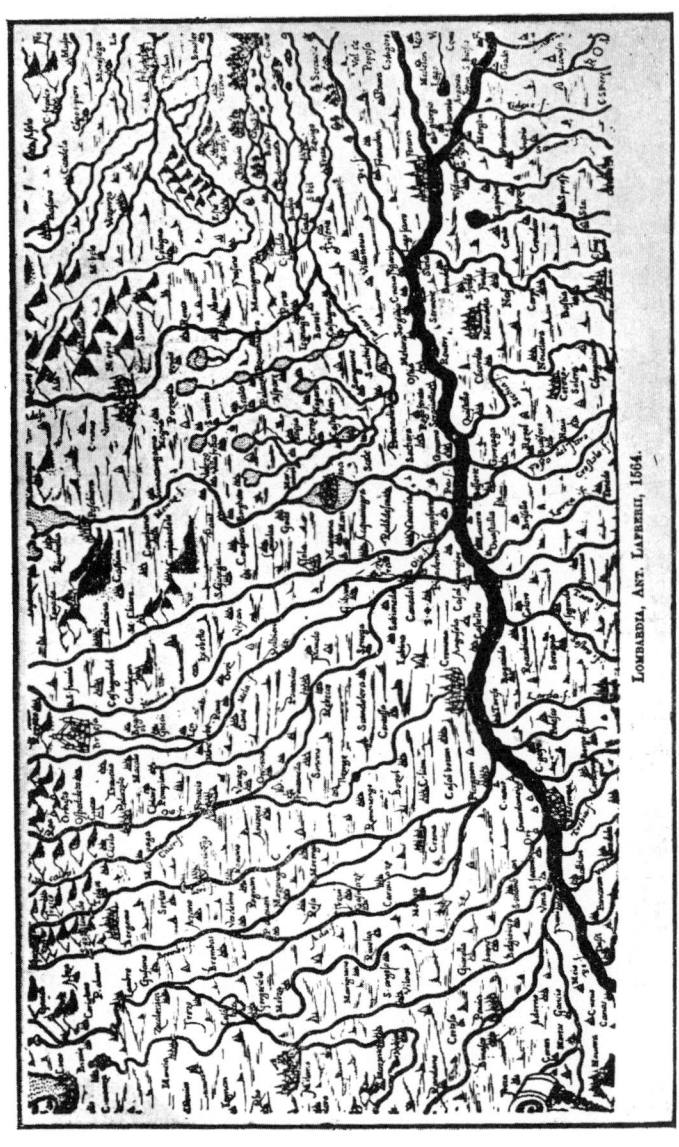

LOMBARDIA, ANT. LAFRERII, 1564.